Mary's Story

Mary's Story

Memoirs of Mary Eliza Leonard Leaman
Compiled by her great-grand daughter,
Eileen Gilligan McKeag Carlyle

© 2017 Mary Eliza Leonard Leaman

ISBN: 1547203765
ISBN 13: 9781547203765

Prologue

Follow Mary Eliza as she journeys westward with her parents in a covered wagon in the mid-1800's. There are encounters with Indians, wild animals and deaths along the trail. Together with her brother and sister, Will and Margaret and their parents, Jacob and Catherine Leonard, they reached their destination of the village of Freeman in Iowa on June 16, 1857. Mary was just three years old when she began this journey. As an adult she recollected these events. These memories are in her own words. This compiled memoir includes not only her own recollections, but is brought to completion by the inclusion of personal hand written letters which she had sent her children and grandchildren during the rest of her life. These family members: her son, Charles D., his wife, Lucile, granddaughters, Mary Jane and Betty June had kept these letters and passed them on for all these years. In those letters she had stated many times that she wished to continue writing down all the history she had lived through and to publish it in book form for her descendants. She handwrote all her memories, but due to declining health, age and lack of a typewriter she was unable to publish her book.

 "MARY'S STORY" has come to life at last. The story includes not only the contents of the hand-written journals she kept, but also includes the loving and informative contents of the letters she wrote to her children during all her years. Combined with Charles City Press articles, either written by her or about her, I was able to put together a compilation of Mary's life and journey in this memoir entitled **"MARY'S STORY."**

 Tales of Indian encounters, the building of a new town, Charles City, and her mother's recollections of the Civil War are included in this exciting book. Mary Leaman even goes as far as to contrast some of her families' Civil War experiences and recollections to the writings of Margaret Mitchell in "**Gone**

with the Wind." Mary Eliza Leonard Leaman grew up, married and had seven children. Come along for this bumpy, dusty and exciting covered wagon journey with Mary as she grows into adulthood and shares her tales of times past.

Eileen Carlyle

Acknowledgements

Where to begin? So many friends, relatives and yes, even doctors encouraged me along the way. They knew that my quest to get this book put together and published was on my "bucket list" so to speak. I had accumulated and stored all this info way too long. I needed to get to work and finish it.

First of all, thanks to my late husband, Roger, who was involved with the early preliminary planning. He didn't realize that the files and boxes he was carting around all those years were Mary's journals, old family letters and photos. He read the early manuscripts and encouraged me. He helped sort photos and old newspaper clippings. He never did see the project to its completion or anywhere near it, but his fingerprints are all over it.

Thanks to my new friend, Veda Baldwin, without whom I can honestly say I could not or would not have completed this project. She encouraged me in the final days. Due to my own health problems I was losing momentum and taking my eyes off the goal: bringing Mary back to life on the pages of this book. It was, after all, "**MARY'S STORY**!"

Veda and I became accustomed to Mary's style of writing, (her numerous commas, run-on sentences and fragmented thoughts!) her appreciation of history and her sense of humor. And as Veda would often exclaim during the final proof readings: "I love this girl!"

Cover photo is of Anna Johnson, great-great-great granddaughter of Mary E. Leaman; she also appears in various places throughout the book in period costume. The other girl seen throughout the book in pioneer attire is Lucy Uhl, another great-great-great granddaughter of Mary E. Leaman.

Thank you also to Colleen Johnson, Anna Johnson, Matthew and Dave Johnson, Scott and Ed McKeag, Connie Janiga, Elaine Mead and Mary Ann Townsend with the Charles City Museum. Thanks also to Max Cargill, for helping with the book cover.

So hopefully, I have brought Mary back to life in the pages of this book. It is Mary that is crossing the Mississippi or looking into the bulging eyes of a charging buffalo on an Iowa prairie. It is Mary that wrote the articles for the local Charles City newspaper.

And so it is, Mary Leonard Leaman, my great grandmother, whom I ultimately thank.

Table of Contents

Prologue · v
Acknowledgements · vii

Chapter 1   Moving By Covered Wagon · · · · · · · · · · · · · · · · · · · 1
Chapter 2   Waiting at the River · 3
Chapter 3   A Death on the Trail · 5
Chapter 4   Crossing the Mississippi River · · · · · · · · · · · · · · · · 6
Chapter 5   Take Me Home! · 9
Chapter 6   A Log House for a Home · 11
Chapter 7   Tribes of Indians · 14
Chapter 8   Mother has a Scare · 16
Chapter 9   Water, Springs and the River · · · · · · · · · · · · · · · · 17
Chapter 10   Buffalo Pursuit · 18
Chapter 11   Electric Storm and Dead Fish · · · · · · · · · · · · · · · 19
Chapter 12   Summer Jaunts · 21
Chapter 13   Bee Trees · 23
Chapter 14   Dangers of Banking · 25
Chapter 15   Cousin Hala Comes to Freeman · · · · · · · · · · · · · 28
Chapter 16   School and the ABC's · 31
Chapter 17   A Rooster Floating By · 34
Chapter 18   From Store to Residence · · · · · · · · · · · · · · · · · · · 36
Chapter 19   Bobtail Cat · 38
Chapter 20   Maple Sugar Time · 39
Chapter 21   Prairie Chickens · 42
Chapter 22   Revenge is Sweet · 43
Chapter 23   Fishing and Hunting Grounds · · · · · · · · · · · · · · 45
Chapter 24   Seeing My First Black Man · · · · · · · · · · · · · · · · · 47

Chapter 25	A Sleigh Ride to Church	50
Chapter 26	Waverly Hill, Strawberries and Snakes	52
Chapter 27	4th of July	55
Chapter 28	Doing Mother's "Calling"	58
Chapter 29	First Kerosene Lamp	62
Chapter 30	Fleeing From the Indians	64
Chapter 31	Indian Scare of 1862	67
Chapter 32	Floyd County's First Courthouse	69
Chapter 33	An Open Air Meeting	71
Chapter 34	Political Meeting	75
Chapter 35	Hiring a New Teacher	77
Chapter 36	Playing a School Trick	80
Chapter 37	Teacher and Cousin Hala	82
Chapter 38	A Nations Loss	85
Chapter 39	We Grow Old	87
	Mary's Personal Correspondence	89
	Newspaper Articles	115
	Newspaper Excerpts from Charles City Press	123
	Family Photographs	127
	Family Obituaries	145
	Genealogy	151

CHAPTER 1

Moving By Covered Wagon

MOTHER'S HEALTH WAS POOR, BEING troubled greatly with asthma. At last the doctor, whose treatment had been ineffectual in her case, advised a change of climate to avoid any pulmonary trouble later on if this was not checked in time. Father acted immediately on his advice. And in company with three of his friends in our neighboring town of Monroe, Wisconsin, who were much interested in the new State of Iowa, started out on a prospecting tour via "covered wagon" to this new state with which they all were favorably impressed.

While he was there, father bought 160 acres near a frontier town which had been platted; consisting of a large log store in which a post office, the first one in what is now Floyd County, had been established. The town was given the founder's name, Freeman. This store was built at the edge of timber to the southwest with a scattering of Burr Oak trees here and there in the open. To the east and south was prairie, except along the river which was fringed with tree fruit in the timber, and also wild game at this time including elk, deer, bear, wild fowl and a small herd of buffalo was a few miles west. A Winnebago Village just to the north of the store was still occupied by the Indians at this time, June 10th, 1856.

When this Government land was put on the market for sale at prices so low that there was a scramble for it despite the Indian scare people took the cheap risk of tomahawks in order to secure for themselves and their families a home. Many Eastern capitalists used their surplus money to tie up much of this valuable land for speculation. They meantime amused themselves in hunting wild game so plentiful in those early days thereby combining business and pleasure. No wonder the wild game soon disappeared and many home seekers were deprived of a chance to acquire good farm land because of these investments.

Father returned to Wisconsin to make preparation for the removal of our family to this new home in what would now seem a wilderness. His occupation from early manhood had been that of farmer in the summer and teacher of the District School in the winter. He taught the two winter terms following his trip to Iowa in what was known as the "Smiley School" near our farm home and in this school house at the end of the last term our household goods were stored until his return from having taken the family to our new home in Iowa.

CHAPTER 2

Waiting at the River

How well we remember our first day on the road. Young though we were, the novelty of riding in a "Covered Wagon" was very interesting. When we stopped for our first meal and mother spread the tablecloth on the prairie grass, placing the bright tin plates and tin cups in lieu of the breakable china. We were thrilled with the newness of it all. Father drove stakes and hung a kettle of water over the fire he had made to heat for tea and coffee. We remember no trees at this place and the cattle had a good feast of the nice prairie grass.

We camped at night when possible where there were trees and water nearby for the stock as well as for ourselves. In a rainy time we tried to reach one of the country taverns to be found along the way where mother with sister, Margaret, and I found shelter, leaving the wagon shelter for Father and Will who needed to be where they could look after the cattle. The sound of the bell worn by one of the cows would warn them if they should wander away. In nice weather Father and Will laid on some blankets under the wagon while Mother with her two little girls slept inside. The black shepherd dog, Ponto, shared with them this shelter while keeping a watchful eye on the cattle that they did not stray away.

How long it took us to reach the Mississippi river I cannot say. I remember having to wait a few days once when what seemed like a whole town of covered wagons waited their turn to be taken across the river. We could not remain in the wagon all the time, and like any restless child I wandered around taking in everything which happened to interest me. It was a motley crowd of people waiting there, many being foreigners whose peculiar clothing attracted my attention, especially the wooden shoes worn by some. I used my eyes to gaze around at the various ones. One woman in particular wearing a heavy quilted skirt with a plain tight-fitting waist with a small, three cornered shawl of bright colors across her shoulders and something on her head turban style was stirring briskly with a wooden paddle which seemed to be some kind of porridge over a camp fire. A few dogs kept coming close sniffing the air that contained the odor which must have been tempting to them. When she seemed to lose patience with the intruders and withdrawing the paddle from the kettle she struck one of them over the back which sent him away howling while the others fled with him. Raising her skirt she wiped the paddle on her blue woolen stocking, returning it to the kettle. We wondered if some dog hair might be clinging to the paddle when she returned it to the kettle and thought "I'm glad I don't have to eat that porridge." My pity for the dogs which I thought might be hungry impressed this on my memory so strongly that this scene remained through all the years.

One day while waiting our turn to be taken across the river, a couple of well-dressed men in a carriage drove up, expecting to be taken across by ferry immediately, but were soon informed they must be placed in line with others and wait their turn, which meant a few days of waiting. Their plight was a sorry one: no shelter, no food, no feed for their horses, and if they turned back to the nearest town or habitation they would again be compelled to wait and what could they do? The ferrymen were determined in their refusal to extend extra favor; they must be fair to people, and have a system in order to avoid any rioting which might otherwise occur. Mother having noticed them talking earnestly with father asked him what the trouble was, and on being informed she said, "We can give them something to eat, if they will accept our simple fare, but you know we can offer them nothing more in the way of accommodations." Father informed them of what mother said, and they must have readily accepted a chance to get something to eat, for they stepped up, politely doffing their hats to her, grateful for that much. Father gave feed to their horses, which he carried for his own, and for the time being they were relieved. They must have bought the chance of the nearest in line to the ferry and got across, as we saw no more of them.

CHAPTER 3

A Death on the Trail

ANOTHER OCCURRENCE WHICH MY BROTHER who was twelve years of age at this time related to me after many years and of which I had no recollection, was the discovery of a woman lying dead in the wagon with a small child clasped in her arms asleep. The mother apparently had passed away while sleeping. The discovery was made by the husband who on looking inside the wagon noticed no sign of breathing, investigated and found his wife had passed on.

Immediately on learning of what had happened the sympathy of all went out to the bereft husband and his little ones. Ready hands came to his assistance in trying to lighten the burden of great sorrow which had come so suddenly upon him and his motherless children. Warm weather and no way of keeping a body meant everything must be done as hurriedly as possible. All were solicited for boards with which to make a coffin. The necessary tools, saws, planes, hammers, nails etc. were collected and deft hands soon had fashioned a coffin. The inside was lined with bed sheets. Sympathetic women prepared the body for burial in a grave which was dug near the bank of the river.

It was decided that Christian burial be given to this unfortunate woman snatched so suddenly from her family. Everyone readily interested themselves in doing all they could to accomplish this. Soon they had found someone to officiate as a minister. With capable ones as a choir and pallbearers, who must carry the coffin to the grave, being no chance of driving any kind of conveyance between those closely arranged wagons. Mother wisely kept us in ignorance of this sad occurrence while father and Will attended the rites without any questioning. Whether my sister Margaret knew of this sad happening I doubt as it never was mentioned. At nightfall the grave had closed over one of the villagers who in the morning had risen in seeming good health and whose family must continue their journey without wife and mother.

CHAPTER 4

Crossing the Mississippi River

BEFORE STARTING OUR TRIP, FATHER had fastened onto the rear end of the wagon, a long narrow box in which were placed six hens and a rooster to make sure of a few chickens on arriving at the new home. There would be no chance to purchase domestic fowls to start with and that was the only sure way to have them. The woods were well stocked with wild fowl but that would not help us in a start of chickens. One day as father was placing some fresh water inside for them, having to loosen a few slats to do so, the rooster in some way made his escape and away he went flapping his wings in his joy of freedom, both running and flying. Soon several dogs in the village of wagons gave chase and where the rooster landed we do not know, perhaps in some one's cook pot. Father was more concerned with keeping the hens from following the lead of the rooster than he was over his loss. The hens were laying one to four eggs each day and were much more worthwhile, and now they would have more room. As darkness came on that night we felt worried over the fate of that rooster, fearing a wolf or a fox might get him, plenty of them around at that time. Whatever his fate, he alone was responsible.

There were people in this village of wagons from all walks of life, but I remember of no disturbance among this motley crowd, each one attending to their own affairs and anxiously awaiting their turn to be taken across the river. Father assisted the ferrymen in many ways, spending much of this time in doing all he could to expedite matters, being very anxious on account of mother's poor health. At last the time arrived when our wagon and one other could be taken across. The teams with their wagons were driven onto the ferry and placed side by side; horses were loosed from the wagons, harnesses removed, halters adjusted and they were driven into the river to swim across with the cattle. Soon the ferry reached the Iowa shore, the horses were caught, harnesses adjusted and again they were hitched to the wagons and driven off the ferry which was now free to return for the next two wagons in the waiting line. This was slow moving to get across the river, but it was the best at that time and may seem incredulous to later generations who were accustomed to bridges of the present spanning these rivers and streams.

Railroads were few west of the Alleghenies and most travel was done by water, then overland by stage or covered wagon. A familiar sight was to see a man with a stick across his shoulder, on which his satchel was hung, cutting across country afoot to reach a desired destination. Today he would be classed "a tramp," then unheard of.

More trials were ahead of us; the worst was yet to come as we soon found out. On nearing the Wapsipinicon River the land seemed to be filled with water underneath, one could see it through the grass, while the wagons would mire down, sometimes hub deep in places. Then father would hand the lines to mother, climb out of the wagon and take fence rails he had placed on the side for emergency, having made a trip prior to this one he knew they would be needed. With the assistance of the man in the rear wagon he pried the wheels up, using some planks as a foundation for them, and then calling to mother to start the horses, sometimes they needed much urging before starting. Well it was that she was skilled in the art of handling horses. When driving or riding on horseback she seemed at perfect ease, handling them in a quiet and seemingly fearless manner. The same thing was done with the team and wagon following ours. This was not the only time we mired down and one can readily understand how necessary it was for two or more wagons to stay close.

Starting on our journey Will had been assigned the duty of cattle driver, but each day father would take his place for a time, giving Will a chance to rest his tired feet and limbs by climbing into the wagon and lying down. Little Ponto, the shepherd dog, took no time off from his job of keeping the cattle together. Ever vigilant in his watchfulness, nipping the heels of any who dared stray off to snatch a mouthful of tempting grass by the wayside, he needed no orders from anyone and the cattle soon learned to keep their place.

When father gave Will his rest from driving the cattle, sister Margaret would take her place on the front seat with Mother and I, where she had a chance to see some of the country through which we were passing, and it was a welcome change to her. Had she not been a great reader of books it would have been more wearisome for her having to sit in the rear of the wagon where she could see but little, jolting along for long hours each day. Sometimes she would stand at the back of the seat, looking over the shoulders of the occupants. She would be looking through the opening of the wagon cover at the rear, watching her brother and little Ponto driving the cattle. Lying down on the bedding for a nap at times, and changing about she whiled away the long hours until time to stop for the night.

CHAPTER 5

Take Me Home!

At last we reached the Wapsipinicon River where there was ferry. A foundation for wagons had been made with heavy brush woven together in some way into a wagon track, and this was held down on the bed of the river by rocks fastened to the edges. This river bottom was treacherous in places and had cost the lives of some unfortunate drivers and their teams in the past. The man or men attending this crossing met us on the shore where we had halted in wait for a pilot. Taking mother, sister and myself in their conveyance, after giving father instructions to drive carefully, directly behind them, keeping closely in the track, the pilot soon had our family safely across and returned to assist the one following us.

We did not go far inland but stopped to camp until the next day. Will had remained on the opposite shore until near evening, when the cattle had quit grazing and were lying down contentedly chewing their cuds. Knowing it was best to leave them where they were for the night, he removed his clothes, rolled them into a tight bundle which he placed across his shoulders, and his heavy leather shoes were carried by fastening the strings around his neck, and with them under his chin he plunged into the murky water of the river and swam across to join the rest of the family. Being an excellent swimmer he had no fear of the water; father having taught him the art of swimming and diving at a very early age, and now those lessons were of great value at this time. The cattle were driven into the river the next morning to swim across and our caravan again started on its journey westward, wallowing over the miry ground, hoping to find a drier place on which to camp that night.

Mother, worn out and wearied with these many trials broke down and cried when we had stopped for the night. A feeling of homesickness had come over her, and in her weakened condition she seemed unable to throw it off. Father, seeing her in tears, took her in his arms and said, "Mother, what is the matter? Why are you crying?" And she replied, "Oh, Jacob! I am so homesick! Take me home!" Tears were in his eyes as he held her to him, this frail wife for whose sake they had left their home and friends in Wisconsin, and while he tried to say comforting and encouraging words to her one could see that he too felt a tinge of homesickness, not knowing what the outcome of this change might be. This soon passed because mother was by nature brave and courageous.

I cannot say how long we were going over what was at that time a quagmire country, but at last we were on solid ground where we could make more miles each day than we had been making over the miry ground, and before nightfall, to the delight and relief of all we drove into the thriving village of Bradford; and a great comfort it was to father and mother to know they now were near their journey's end. Mother was enchanted with the clean looking streets and the beautiful Burr Oak trees. It seemed like heaven to her, following those experiences they had encountered, and she longed to establish a home in this inviting and restful looking place. But father on his previous trip had bought land twelve or thirteen miles further on, expecting to make a home there and this could not well be considered at that time. We remained in Bradford over night, and next morning continued on to our destination.

CHAPTER 6

A Log House for a Home

ON ARRIVING AT FREEMAN, MOTHER alighted from the wagon, looked at the surroundings, drew a breath of satisfaction, for she, like father, was a lover of nature and this place he had chosen for our new home was most beautiful at this time. Plenty of timber to the west, with a small grove to the north, at which place father had stopped the team on our arrival, broad prairie to the south, and to the east was hazel brush across the road from the Freeman log building. The prairie was brilliant with wild flowers, for this was the month of June - the month of roses - and the prairie pinks, or "Sweet Williams" as we called them and the bright red prairie Lilies with many other flowers were growing in profusion. Unmolested, they had blossomed year after year, dropping their seeds to spring up the following summer in their varied colorings more beautiful than ever.

At this time, June 16, 1857, there were but twelve buildings in the village of Freeman, very scattered. Three had been for business and nine remaining ones were residences; some were frame, others were log. The Freeman log store which became our early home, shortly after our arrival, was the first building in what is now Charles City, and in it was the first post office in Floyd County, all mail coming being addressed to "Freeman," brought by stage, and people for miles around got their mail from this frontier post office, and household supplies as well. Some of the shelving still remained when we moved in, though the counters had been removed. A wooden latch, with string hanging out through the day to allow people to come in for their mail and supplies was drawn in at night and the store with its contents was safe from prowlers. This latch looked as though it had been whittled with a jackknife, but it answered the purpose for which it was meant. The door was a wide one with windows on each side to give the needed light; the side walls were windowless and had contained the shelving.

A Winnebago village close by must have furnished some patronage for the store as well as that of the white people, who were constantly passing through seeking homes in the north and west. The small grove at which father stopped the team on our arrival was just northeast of the Freeman store building. Two Burr Oak trees are all that is left of that grove, now facing on Freeman Street. There was hazel brush between the store building and the Hackley house a block east, through which ran a well beaten foot path. Our family had traveled back and forth for our mail and supplies and the path continued to be used by our family and the Hackley's in neighborly visits. A wagon road leading diagonally over the hill, branched off about one block before reaching the Freeman Building, one road leading to the ford, while the other one ran close by the building where the stages had delivered the mail each day then diagonally to the river, turning near the "boiling spring" followed along the river until reaching the approach to the first bayou bridge, continued on the Floyd.

Being unable to secure a house on our arrival we had been compelled to remain in the covered wagon two or three weeks, and it rained much of the time. At last the family occupying the store building, having a house nearly completed a short distance away, kindly offered the use of one half the building to our family. It was thankfully accepted and greatly appreciated by mother who had been compelled to cook our meals over a smoldering campfire of wet fuel. There was only one bakery where we purchased our bread, no meat market, and we still had to use the salt meat we had 4brought with us. But we enjoyed plenty of fish with which the river was well stocked, and with plenty of wild fowl to be had, one could live very well when they could have a cook stove on which to do their cooking.

Every evening the singing of the Whippoorwill and the call of Bobwhite, the dainty quail running around seemingly with no fear, while the hooting of a family of owls which had established a home in some nearby trees, furnished plenty of entertainment at night. The howling of the prairie wolves nearby and the timber wolves farther down the river, as well as the "Catamounts" - a panther-like animal whose cry was like that of person in distress - caused us to nestle close to father, taking refuge between his knees, our back against his breast, and so long as we had him at our back we fearlessly faced all danger.

We sat outside evenings when the weather permitted, but mother wisely remained inside to avoid the mosquitoes singing around ones ears. Sometimes father would build a smoldering fire - more smoke than blaze - he called it a "smudge", and that kept them away pretty well; it seemed more pleasant outside on a summer evening with so much to interest one.

CHAPTER 7

Tribes of Indians

DIFFERENT TRIBES OF INDIANS WERE often passing through, and the building we occupied being on the direct route they were sure to stop, always wanting something, and being very insistent in their demands, sometimes complied with and then again it would be necessary to refuse them. As an example, a mother hen was passing through the yard with her brood, clucking in motherly fashion, when the Indian acting as spokesman for the tribe demanded the baby chickens - about the size of a sparrow. Mother was disgusted and said "No! One would not make a mouthful, you can't have them." She never sent them away empty handed, but would always give them some sort of food. Sometimes it would be cornbread left over from dinner, and some meat - salt of course. They motioned as though to spread butter and mother answered, "I am out of butter," and I think she was. The squaws did not always dismount, remaining on their ponies, though if they did they would come inside the house, peering into everything and helping themselves to anything they might want. One needed to keep their eyes open when they called.

The Winnebago Indians were inclined to be friendly and as this had been their former home, one they seemed to have loved, they kept returning at intervals to their old haunts. Fishing was good, wild game plenty, and the site of their former village seemed irresistible to them. Father called two of the Indians by name; one he called "Bradford," and the other one "Jim". I do not know what their Indian names were. They seemed to be able to understand and talk some of the "white man's" language, much more than any of the other tribes that called.

Knowing their habits, we children on seeing a band of Indians coming over the hill would scurry into the house with the announcement, "The Indians are coming!" at which mother would busy herself hiding everything she thought might attract them, but they were sure to see something for which they would beg.

One of these visits I always will remember. Mother was confined to her bed and this time the Indians came unexpectedly and the first thing their eyes rested on was a bunch of peacock feathers which she had brought from our Wisconsin home; having kept them for sentimental reasons. Immediately they began begging for them; surrounding her bed, while we children were huddled nearby looking on. Being very insistent in their demands for the feathers and Mother fearing to anger them after they had held out silver pieces to her said: "I do not wish to sell them, they are a keepsake, but you may have a few of them." Immediately they made a dive for them and it was a sorry looking bunch of feathers when they were through with them.

They were in camp on the north side of the river, and some of the townsmen had persuaded them to give an entertainment in the stone hall, and they wished to decorate their heads in true Indian style; the peacock feathers being very appropriate for the occasion. Later on at night when they had concluded their performance they crossed the river to the site of their former village, and close to a large Burr Oak tree, which stood in the open not far from the "Boiling Spring", they made a fire around which they danced chanting their Indian Song.

The noise had attracted us, sister and I, and we stepped outside to see what it was all about. Leaning against the side of the house, where the Indians were in full view - though they could not see us - we watched their performance. As they danced around the fire they would motion with their tomahawks as though to strike each other; continuing the performance until the fire had burned low, when they re-crossed the river to join the rest of their tribe. The

show was over and no one had witnessed it but two little girls who took it all in while the Indians were unaware they had an audience.

Next morning we went to the site of their performance and found scattered around the burnt embers of their fire Mother's highly prized peacock feathers, many with the stem broken. We gathered up all those worthwhile and carried them home to her.

CHAPTER 8

Mother has a Scare

MOTHER STEPPED OUTSIDE ONE EVENING as Father sat reading, and soon rushed in exclaiming: "Jacob! There is something out there. I reached my hand under the wagon and felt f-u-r-r!" He immediately lit the candle in the tin lantern and went out to investigate, returning in a very few moments. Mother asked, "Jacob, what was it?" and with a smile answered; "Nothing but a couple of bears taking a snooze. They'll do no harm."

With no windows on the side walls of the building, a stable door securely fastened and a strong high board fence enclosing the cows and pigs, who were safe from molestation. In addition father's gun rested on two forked sticks fastened to the kitchen wall near the stove with the powder horn hanging by a strap beneath. On a shelf above was a metal flask containing shot and his outfit for molding bullets, all of which were kept in a readiness for time of need. It was an interesting time for us when he would be molding bullets before the kitchen stove or Mother "running candles", sometimes allowing us to hold the stick to which the wicks were fastened, while she poured the melted tallow, and always with the injunction; "Now hold it steady," which we tried to do. The next morning the bears were gone.

CHAPTER 9

Water, Springs and the River

I WOULD NOT MISS GIVING a description of the wonderful "Boiling Spring" of early days and for some years following. It was a beautiful sight. The stage would sometimes halt in its travel along the river to give the passengers a chance to view this wonderful spring. The force of the vein of water from which it was fed being so strong, caused it to bubble up geyser-fashion to at least eight to ten inches.

No wells were here at first as those living anywhere near the river on the Freeman side would have to go through many feet of limestone rock and it seemed as though nature had provided those wonderful springs because of this. Much shade there was from the boughs of a graceful elm just above the spring reaching out its branches as though to protect it while extending out into the river some distance were smooth flat rocks of a very hard substance on which we children would sometimes play. Often in the early morning, the snipe, dozens of them, would be walking around near the water catching minnows for their breakfast and they got plenty of them.

There were no bridges at this time and the Lamborn boys, stepsons of Mr. Hackley, kept a boat at the ford taking people across charging five cents one way or ten cents for the round trip. There was a ferry above a log dam but was not used much for foot passengers, being more expensive. Sometimes one could cross on the log dam when the water was low, walk on some planks laid across the mill-race and land on the opposite shore where all the business and the people had to cross the river for their supplies. Father generally stocked up on our household supplies. Then in times of high water, as sometimes happened, we were prepared.

CHAPTER 10

Buffalo Pursuit

SHORTLY AFTER WE HAD MOVED into the Freeman store building and while the Richard Cummings family still was there, their son Johnny, near my age, and his brother Willie and myself were sitting in the door yard (no fence around the place then) when suddenly we heard a crackling of bushes, beating of hooves and shouting of horsemen. Turning my head in the direction of the sounds, I found myself looking into the bulging eyes of a buffalo which threw up its front feet directly for my head while the other two or more scattered out. We watched them as they went tearing over the prairie with shouting horsemen after them, one with a rope or lasso coiled around his saddle horn. We presume it was Mr. Bigelow himself, as he had been gathering animals for an eastern menagerie. The buffalo had in some way broken out of the log building in which they together with some bears, elk, deer and other animals he had collected were kept. We will always believe that our sitting quietly, more surprised than frightened, saved our lives; for had we screamed and tried to scramble up there was no telling what the end of this little drama might have been. Fortunately we were not easily frightened. This little scene happened in the dooryard of the cottage which stands on the exact spot once occupied by the Freeman store on what is now Hildreth Street.

What went on inside the house while this was happening? My sister Margaret, who was inside with Mother, said "Mother saw it just as the buffalo was upon you and fainted, falling to the floor." Hard on sister, she it was who needed the sympathy as she had the job of reviving Mother with no one nearby to assist her. Mrs. Cummings was, perhaps at the new house they were building as I have no recollection of her being present when this exciting scene transpired.

CHAPTER 11

Electric Storm and Dead Fish

THE CEDAR RIVER WAS A beautiful stream in the early days with a fringe of trees along its bank on the Freeman side, with grapevines hanging from many of them, and Blackhaws and Thornapples adding to its beauty. At the right, just before reaching the ford was a tall Basswood, the "Hackley Spring", boxed in with heavy plank to keep stock which ran loose from tramping in it. A Rivulet running from the spring to the river sparkled in the sunlight and its clean sandy bottom added to its beauty. There were several other large trees beside smaller ones among which, in their season, we gathered many wild flowers, Dutchman's Breeches, bloodroot, etc.

This was in and around the present electric power house site. There was no rock until one approached the ford where the bank on your left was the beginning of the limestone bank, more in evidence as you neared the "boiling spring." The bank of the river at the power house site and nearby was all a black loam soil, no rock in sight. What one now sees and for many years past was hauled in and a kiln for burning lime was built in the black loamy bank where those wildflowers had grown so plentifully. Trees were felled, rock hauled in and the place so changed one who had not seen it as nature made it, could not imagine the change.

During the first summer of our arrival, my brother whose duty is was to procure fresh water in preparation for breakfast, returned from the spring with the water and said, "Father, do you know those flat rocks down by the spring are covered with dead fish?" Well, that needed investigating! Taking a good sized washtub he and Will returned and in a very short time came back with the tub full of fish, all sorts and sizes. Not wanting to leave any to putrefy near the spring they gathered them all regardless of size. They sorted them after they got home; giving the suckers to the pigs and dividing with the neighbors the more choice ones and all had nice fish fries. The theory arrived at for this phenomenon was that a heavy electrical storm had occurred during the night with some fearful flashes. It was thought that lightning must have struck the water throwing the fish unto the flat rocks where they were found still nice and fresh, this being very early in the morning. Many choice fish were among them, such as pickerel and black bass.

CHAPTER 12

Summer Jaunts

On Sunday afternoons during our first summer in Iowa, Father would hitch his team to the wagon and take us for an outing always driving on the south road first, for a visit to the wild prairie land he had purchased on his first trip out here in 1856, expecting at that time to establish our home there. The prairie was gorgeous with its abundance of wild flowers and looked beautiful to us as we eagerly gathered them by the handfuls while Father and Mother were looking around planning where it was best to place the buildings.

Mother was very happy at the thought of another farm home. She loved country life and was pleased with the land he had chosen. It was gently rolling, just enough so for necessary drainage with a pebbly bottomed spring of clear cold water and from this was to be seen a stream flowing into the creek. A lone Elm tree stood a few feet to the west, its graceful boughs spreading as though to shade the portion of the creek from the sun's rays. Mother pointed out where she wanted the milk house located so that the stream of cold water would be flowing through it. Everything looked perfect to Mother.

Time was passing rapidly and Father thought we had better be starting if we were to go across the river into the timber to search for bee trees to replenish our diminishing supply of honey. He drove east and southeast for some distance turning into the first road leading to the river, known as "Lambert's Ford." Reaching the water's edge he suddenly stopped the team. Seeing at his left a large tree lying in the river having been felled by the gnawing of beavers, who were now busily building their winter home, usually called a beaver dam. They did not halt their work at our approach, seeming to ignore our presence, but kept right on with their labor. The larger one of the group was doing the hauling of the mortar which had been piled on his flat tail by the mortar mixers who seemed to know their business. He then traveled along on the body of the tree with his load until he reached a certain point where it was unloaded by the others. The mortar they were mixing was composed of a clay-like substance they gathered on the bank of the river nearby. This would hold together when the ordinary black soil, containing as it does more or less sand, would be washed away by the water. Wise little animals they are! There we learned why nature made a beaver's tail so broad and flat and the meaning of the phrase "working like beavers." We now understood. Seeing them as we did at their work was an encyclopedia on their habits and we learned something we never forgot. We watched them for some time at their mixing, loading and unloading until the one doing the hauling had made three trips. We drove across the river where we found nothing as interesting as the beavers. I have often wondered what became of the little fellows. Perhaps they were killed by some hunter for their pelts of valuable fur. This occurrence was in the summer of 1857 and I have never seen a beaver since.

CHAPTER 13

Bee Trees

ON THESE EXCURSIONS TO THE timber, Father always placed a large tin pail in the wagon to contain whatever we found worth taking home. We always found something worthwhile, but honey was hoped for this day. Mother was left as driver of the team while Father skirmished around looking for bee trees. Presently his "hoo-hoo" call was to tell us that he had located one. She started the team in the direction of the call winding among the trees in a zigzag fashion to reach him. A less courageous woman would have hesitated at being left as driver but she possessed a true pioneer spirit and was unacquainted with the word "can't." Father knew that, otherwise he would have returned to do the driving himself. When we reached him he was standing by the tree studying how best to get at the honey. There was no thought of cutting the tree with such an abundance of honey as the timber was not his.

Finally he had figured out a way which took some climbing, so he fastened a rope to his pail, threw it over his arm and began the climb to a point he thought would best enable him to secure the supply. Looping the rope until he had drawn the pail up within his reach he fastened it securely to the limb of the tree and began scooping the honey out with a long handled skimmer. The pail was soon filled with luscious sweetness. The bees could easily gather their sweets from Basswood buds and the great variety of wild blossoms to be found, saying nothing of the many other sources of supply. This wild honey had the most delicious flavor to it and I have never enjoyed the taste of honey as I did then; it is like the maple sugar.

Father carefully lowered the pail to the ground, Mother placing it so it would not tip. He then unfastened the rope from the limb, gave it a toss and was soon on the ground, pretty well out of breath. It had been strenuous work but he felt well paid. The pail of honey was placed in the wagon, secured from tipping, covered over and the return journey home was begun. Father did the driving zigzagging through the trees until he could make a turn. We soon reached the road leading to the river where he stopped to allow the horses to drink. It was now late and we did not stop again even to watch the beavers still busy at work. The afternoon had been one of pleasure as well as profit and all were happy even though tired.

Mother afterward strained much of the honey from the comb using the latter for bees wax. She melted this comb, I think, by placing it in a basin or pan which she set in hot water to dissolve it. Beeswax was considered essential for waxing the thread in hand sewing, especially for men's clothing. This kept the thread from tangling as one sewed. Sewing machines were here at this time but most sewing was done by hand. Many little tooth marks were found on Mother's ball of beeswax as we children used it for chewing gum.

The honey was much nicer for the table after having been strained from the comb. A pitcher was used to contain it and it was easily served. I will never forget the delicious taste of that wild honey purchased with no cost except labor.

I remember of no interference from the bees while the honey was being procured. Every available space in this tree had been filled and we thought the bees had swarmed as they often do to find other quarters in which to continue their labor. Working bees never retire, no matter how rich their store of honey may be they still continue their labor. In fact, they work themselves to death in their short span of life, said to be but six weeks, leaving the fruit of their labor to others. They had no time for the drones. No matter how much money they have in store, their rule seems to be: "If you don't work, you don't eat." A drone never works, living on the labor of others. The queen is busy producing the eggs from which a swarm is hatched every six weeks, earning her right to exist. How long her span of life is we cannot say, but it is a useful one.

CHAPTER 14

Dangers of Banking

NO BANK HAD BEEN ESTABLISHED at the time our family arrived in 1857, and not until some years later. One or more persons having money did some private banking, making loans at an exorbitant rate of interest. No money except gold and silver was then in use, and this was not easily transported across country by team or on horseback to or from the nearest express office at the terminal of the railroad, and was fraught with much danger for anyone so employed.

At one time father was to return from one of his regular trips bringing quite a sum of money from the express office for one of the merchants here. Realizing the risk he was taking he meant to use every precaution in doing so. Passing in and out of the depot platform were some questionable looking characters. Knowing he was expected to take the money up with him that night - this was late afternoon - he meant to use every precaution. Imagine the shock when the express agent called out to him and asked: "Are you going to take that money up with you tonight?" "I'm not" father answered in not a very mild tone, though he intended doing so knowing it would be expected. Watching for a chance when he thought the crowd had dispersed he went to the express agent, secured the money and started on his return journey.

An eighteen year old boy was his only company on this trip and they had a long drive through some heavily timbered country before reaching one of the taverns where they planned to spend the night. At other times when the weather was fair they would camp at some point along the way, saving their hotel bill. No camping was contemplated that night and they drove along at a brisk pace, the boy's team in advance. While going through the most heavily timbered part of the road the boy's team suddenly stopped. Father being anxious to reach the tavern soon as possible called to the boy and asked: "What is the matter, Gene? Why are you stopping?" There was no answer and the advance team again started up. After driving some distance it again stopped. Divining something must be wrong, father hopped out of his wagon, withdrew his gun which he always carried on his trips for safety. Just then two men made for the timber and disappeared in the darkness. Father and the boy continued their drive without further happenings until they reached the tavern where they stopped for the night, and the next morning continued on their homeward journey. Horse thieving at that time made it necessary for a man when on the road to carry a gun for protection to himself and his team.

At another time father was to carry with him for this same merchant a large sum of money to the nearest express office which was then at Cedar Falls. They made arrangements for delivering the money to father the night before he was to leave on his trip, and mother was informed of their plans. When father answered a rapping at the door about 9:30 o'clock that night she sat quietly with her knitting, taking no notice of the visitor he admitted, while we children looked on in wonderment when a man wearing a long, black circular cloak reaching to his instep, and his hat closely concealing his face came inside. No word was spoken by anyone and the man walked to the large clock on the wall and opening the door placed inside a buckskin bag full of gold and silver money, though at the time we did not know what the bag contained. Then he passed out of the door without having been recognized by any of the children, a thing hoped for. Father left early the next morning for Cedar Falls and the mysterious bag the man placed in the clock the night before went with him.

The country was sparsely settled, the roads were poor and the carrying of a large sum of money was not a desirable job for anyone, and was dangerous for those employed. Father faced all these dangers until the Illinois Central, the first railroad to reach Charles City, arrived September 12, 1868, when he established the first dray line. The Chicago, Milwaukee and St. Paul followed.

Both men and women in the early days showed little fear and we have often wondered at the nerve they displayed when confronted with danger. I never saw mother show fear when visited by Indians as we often were, with father absent and only her and us children at home. If she felt a fear, her looks did not betray it. People at the present time have little idea what the early pioneers endured.

CHAPTER 15

Cousin Hala Comes to Freeman

IN THE AUTUMN OF 1858 our family made a trip to southern Iowa to bring father's niece, whose mother had died, home with us. Father feared a second trip in little more than a year after the one we had made from Wisconsin would be too much for Mother, who was not strong, but she said "Jacob, I cannot sleep at night with worry over Sally's child being left with strangers. We must go after her." So a second trip was made, via "covered wagon" the only recourse at the time.

Roads were much better than the ones we had come over from Wisconsin on reaching eastern Iowa, and not being burdened with live stock we traveled right along and this journey was a pleasant one and much quicker made. Soon we reached grandfather's place at Fairfield where we visited a few days before going after father's niece. The people with whom she lived had been kind to her and wished to keep her, having no daughter of their own, but their home was remote from school and her chance of an education was very meager. This had been a worry to her relatives who urged father and mother to come and get her. She had but a dim recollection of this uncle and aunt, who did not want to take her away with them unless she chose to go, but the chance to visit at grandfathers was a great inducement to her and she very willingly accompanied us.

Mother wished to visit an uncle in Mount Pleasant before returning home, and Hala was left at grandfathers where she loved to be, until our return. During our visit at Mount Pleasant, mother's uncle gave all the time he could spare from his patients (being a physician) showing places he thought might be of interest to father and mother. I was too young to be much interested in everything we saw, but I remember the visit to the Insane Asylum, then nearing completion. Perhaps because of getting so tired from walking up and down the long flights of stairs, and the distance through one hall seemed endless. Doors were on each side of this hall but I do not remember of any being opened and it seems to me there was the smell of fresh paint. I doubt if there were any patients confined there at this time - September or October 1858.

On returning from this visit to Mount Pleasant we did not remain long at Grandfather's as father wished to reach home in time to prepare for the coming winter. We were soon on the road, accompanied by Hale, who seemed glad to go with us. I remember of no bad weather and the return trip was a pleasant one. My brother, sister and cousin would often walk quite a distance when on the prairie to rest themselves from sitting in the wagon where they could see but little, amusing themselves gathering the fall flowers.

One place I remember was going through heavy timber, a rail fence between it and the road, with elk and deer looking out at us. Father stopped the team to allow all who wished to pick up the bright, shiny buckeyes lying around. I do not remember what part of Iowa this was as I was too young to be geographically interested. The big trees I have always loved; the elk and deer looking out upon us and the bright buckeyes scattered around is one of the memory pictures still with me.

We arrived home safely and Hala seemed very content and happy. She and sister, Margaret, though some years younger were real companions to each other and many happy years were spent together. Mother loved this orphaned niece and I think that love was reciprocated.

The years passed, Hala attended school, later on taught school for some time and finally was married to a very estimable and promising young man. Many years later, in her old age, I visited her and while reminiscing about events of those early days she said "I walked in with the rest of the family and never for a moment during all the years did I feel that I was not one of them." Then sitting quietly for a few moments in deep thought, she said "Dear Aunt Cass!" It was a way she always had shown toward me that caused me to feel the confidence and freedom of an own child, I did not realize in my younger days all it meant to me, but have thought of it many times in later years."

This cousin was very dear to all of our family. All are now gone from earthly scenes of the family in which she was reared, and she too, with her dear husband and three sons, have "crossed the bar" and we often wonder if we'll know each other there?

CHAPTER 16
School and the ABC's

A SCHOOL HOUSE HAD BEEN built on the north side of the river and the few children in Freeman at that time would cross the river by boat or on the ice when the river was frozen over enough to be safe. This was not very satisfactory as much time was lost when conditions were unfavorable. People were coming in great numbers, some of them locating on farms close by and many of them with large families.

The nearest school to the south side was the Humphrey School, now known as the Lane School about five miles south of Freeman. As a beginning, a winter term of school (1858-59) was held in the Hackley residence. We cannot recall the name of the teacher but think it was the Rev. Windsor. However, the following summer school was taught in the Brayton house on what is now South Iowa Street. The teacher was Miss Lucy Carver. One term sufficed Miss Carver, she having decided a school of one scholar was to be preferred. Our next teacher was J. Cheston Whitney who taught the winter term of 1859-60. Their family lived upstairs. Meanwhile the school patrons had decided on building a schoolhouse in District No. 2. They purchased ground from Mr. Harvey Kellog Sr. on Rockford Road just one block west of South Main Street. They built a very nice school house we thought but soon it was crowded beyond comfort. Mr. Whitney proved to be a very efficient and competent teacher. Two years later patrons and students regretted his resignation; he had decided on other fields of occupation.

This was before Charles City had a graded school system. It was difficult for any teacher having scholars from the first primary (or kindergarten) to the grow-ups studying the higher academic branches. It certainly was a test of ability.

It had been planned to start me in school when the summer term began. My brother, Will, had been assigned the job of teaching me the alphabet during the winter working with me each afternoon. Mother was too busy sewing by hand for the family. This was before the newly invented sewing machine by Silas Howe had reached this country. Making a new dress, even for a child, was slow work. Mother had in readiness for one important day a brown dress with small white polka dots and a new pair of shoes, both a delight to my childhood fancy.

These ABC lessons were given as we say by a table facing the west window of the kitchen. The bright afternoon sun was shining in and the new primer with the alphabet and pictures so attractive to me. Will began his teaching by pointing with his lead pencil to each letter in rotation A,B,C,D,E,F, etc. with me repeating after him. Things went well with these lessons and his pupil seemed apt until he began skipping around. Then the "tug of war" began and I was unable to recall the names of all those queerly shaped letters. In despair he laid the pencil down and said to Mother: "This young'n doesn't know anything!" Again taking up the pencil and pointing to the baffling letter A, he said "Now say A!" I immediately repeated after him "Now say A" bobbing my head to give vehemence to the fact he closed his mouth tightly, looked at me a moment as though more convinced than ever that Mary didn't know anything. I began to wonder though nothing was said. Then I remembered that polka dot dress and the new shoes. I tried again. At last one of the little brain cells must have opened for soon I was able to distinguish each of those puzzling letters, recall their names, and the alphabet battle was over and won.

Then came the lessons in spelling: _ax, _ox, etc., to begin and soon I was progressing finely. Will was encouraged with the advancement of his pupil who now had no need of a "dunce cap." Next I must learn to count to one hundred and then I would be ready to start school. This accomplished, I felt myself very important. This method, now obsolete, would be very puzzling to both teachers and pupils at the present time but in the long ago it was considered very essential.

I recall an instance many years later where a couple having started their little son in school and being anxious to know how he was progressing, they asked him to bring his book home so that they might know how much he had learned. The little fellow did so gladly. Opening his book at the day's lesson and with all assurance began reading giving the sounds instead of the name of each letter. Horrified, the father stopped him and next morning accompanied him to school to demand an explanation of this "crazy method." On the way he stopped at our house to tell us of his grievance and remarked "What am I paying taxes for, to pay teachers for making a fool of my boy? I guess not!" His wrath was in summer heat as he went on with his "hopeful." This was the Pollard method, just introduced into our schools. This lad is now a grandfather and I am wondering if he remembers this?

When the summer term started I was in attendance as had been planned, walking quite a distance each day with my sister Margaret, cousin Hala, and brother Will. My brother had labored so hard to prepare me for the event. Most vividly, however, I remember the abundance of wild flowers, the prairie grass, and the whir of the prairie chickens' wings as they flew up on our approach and the singing of the meadow larks. There was dew on the grass sparkling in the bright sunlight and a creek we must cross on our way. The girls would remove their shoes and stockings, to wade across the creek. One of the larger boys carried me on his back. Things have greatly changed since then with the cultivation of prairie land, drainage ditches, etc., and those places are well dried out. This road we traveled was across unbroken prairie between the Perry farm and the Humphrey School, now known as the Lane School. In this building some years later Carrie Lane, now Mrs. Catt, received the first few years of her education.

**Aa Bb Cc Dd Ee Ff Gg Hh Ii Jj Kk Ll Mm
Nn Oo Pp Qq Rr Ss Tt Uu Vv Ww Xx Yy Zz**

CHAPTER 17

A Rooster Floating By

During the early sixties, a freshet occurred caused by excessive rainfalls swelling the many streams flowing into the Cedar River which had overflowed its banks. Think it must have been during the month of June as the trees were in full leaf. Much debris was floating down the river, fallen trees, logs, boards and all kinds of rubbish washed from the banks, including some dead animals as well. The most interesting thing seen floating down was a large tree in full leaf, standing upright, and as it neared the log dam, a small dark object was seen on one of its lower limbs. On reaching the dam the tree swayed for an instant then came over the dam carrying with it several of the logs and landed upright in the foaming water below. Just then that small dark object which proved to be a rooster, flapped his wings and crowed loudly several times, whether from joy over his safe descent or from fright and nervousness, I do not know. The tree went sailing majestically on with its feathered passenger still on board, flapping his wings and crowing. Well it was that no bridge was here at this time; it certainly would have been disastrous for the bridge, the tree being a large one, and the rooster most likely would have found a watery grave.

The passenger was still on board as the tree went out of sight, and we were hoping it might land at some point projecting out into the water, enabling the rooster to fly to dry land. Still danger would be confronting him, the country being infested by wolves and foxes, his prospects of safety were not very bright. We still had hope the landing would be near a farm yard, though we knew the farms were few and far between, but we still hoped all might be well for the unfortunate fowl. Each night on going to bed we would lie

awake for a time, wondering and hoping that all was well for the rooster carried downstream against his will. The tree must have dropped into the river during the night when the soil which had held it was washed away by the water, and it must have come from a distance. Had it started at crowing time, the rooster certainly would have flown to land and safety. Poor unfortunate bird.

CHAPTER 18

From Store to Residence

S.C. GODDARD BUILT THE FIRST frame store building in what was then the village of Freeman. This building was in the northwest corner of the block east of where the McKinley school now is. It was a general store which he afterward sold in 1856 and built the Magnolia Hotel on the north side of the river which was consumed with fire. After business was no longer carried on in Freeman, this store building was used for residential purpose (as I have mentioned before) being often tenanted by two or three families at one time. The Miles Waller family being the first to occupy it until their residence, the first one, which was on the north side of the river was ready for occupancy.

For a time, H. Kannengeiser started in the furniture business in this building, the family residing upstairs. They had come from New York, I think, and lost one of their children (a babe) while occupying the Goddard store. Freeman seemed a poor place for business now that both the flour mill and saw mill were on the north side. Mr. Kannengeiser later secured a building in the block facing the city park, continuing in business until his death. The store continued to be used for residential purposes by many families until they could build a house and they were glad for the shelter as there were no homes for sale at this time. The counters were still in place, also the shelving, both of which were put to good use, the counters serving for dining table, etc. This had been a well built store and was very nice for that early day. Within its walls, while still used as a general store was an occurrence too ludicrous to pass by unmentioned.

An election for a new postmaster was arranged to be held there and both Democratic and Republicans had chosen candidates. Voters of both parties from far and near were present. The momentous time arrived and having no ballot box a plug hat was used. All went well until in counting votes it was discovered the Democratic candidate had more votes than there were voters all told and the question: "Who has been stuffing the ballot box?" arose. Accusations were made and indignantly denied of course. When things waxed hot, someone blew out the candles not wanting this election to end in a blood riot. Candidates and voters had to grope their way out in the dark as best they could. Needless to say, we were not present when this transpired. It was handed down to us and came to my mind when the returns of our last presidential election were given in 1932.

CHAPTER 19

Bobtail Cat

In the grove facing this store through which we were returning home from play with the children near nightfall, birds were twittering from their roosting places in the trees. We happened to glance up over our shoulder and just above us on the limb of the tree was the largest cat we had ever seen except in captivity. Being especially fond of the feline family we halted and began calling" "Kitty, kitty, kitty." As we started in a second time with the calling it slowly turned his head in our direction showing plainly its broad face, short ears and then we noticed lastly its bob-tail. Do not think we tarried! We covered the ground as fast as our limbs could carry us. He was not the cat whose acquaintance we cared to make.

CHAPTER 20

Maple Sugar Time

In the early spring of 1859, father took over the management of the John Perry farm in Riverton Township, during Mr. Perry's absence to Pike's Peak (Black Hills) on a gold quest. Our family moved from the Freeman log store building to his farm into the large log house, on which had been added a smaller frame one for Mrs. Perry and her three children. Having someone close by during his absence gave her a feeling of security, and was less worry to him on having to leave them alone while he was away from home.

Bands of Indians were frequently passing through, and the added fear of wild animals, with which the country was infested, meant something to a lone woman; the noises made by the different animals at night gave one a creepy feeling. So much heavy timber along the river made it conducive for their needs, where they could prey on each other to their hearts content. Timber Wolves, Panthers, or should I call them Cougars; whatever, the noise they made sounded like someone in distress. The howling of Timber Wolves, as well as Prairie Wolves, furnished plenty of nightly entertainment. In my childish fear of these noises I had adopted the habit of covering my head with bedclothes at night, and in warm weather almost smothered myself.

Mr. Perry had acquired a number of acres of timber along the river to furnish their fuel, etc. There was much hard maple from which could be secured the sugar water for sugar making. The maple sugar was used to sweeten the wild fruit so plentiful then, and was also used for cake making. Very little white sugar was used by anyone, except in the sugar bowl for tea and coffee. The common brown sugar went into the manufacture of cookies, cakes, etc., except on rare occasions, while those having their own maple sugar used it instead of the brown sugar which they had to buy.

Now maple sugar is a great luxury, and rarely do we find the pure maple; invariably it is adulterated, and I seldom indulge - the disappointment is too great. I lived in the early days. All fruit was either dried or preserved. No such thing as glass fruit jars had been introduced in this part of the country at this time, though they were patented in the late fifties. Canned fruit and vegetables were unknown in those early days.

When sugar water began to run in the maple trees, father made preparations to make sugar and syrup during the time it would be running. A soft snow had fallen after the breakup of winter, called a "sugar snow." Father crossed the river in a boat to investigate, found the sugar water had commenced to run and made immediate preparation for sugar making, and Will was kept out of school to assist him.

The camp was provided with all the needful things for sugar making. A fire place built of stone on which a large iron vat holding many gallons was placed; wooden pails to catch the sugar water as it ran from the trees through spouts, made of sumac limbs. The spouts were inserted by first boring a hole with a small auger, and after the sugar water had ceased to run the holes were closed up to avoid injury to the trees. If I remember rightly, two holes were bored in each tree, on opposite sides that is, one hole in each side. During the time the sugar water was running father would start with two empty pails, visiting each tree until the pails were full, then return to the fireplace and pour the sugar water into the vat which he kept closely covered to avoid dirt and dust that might fall in. This kept him busy visiting the many trees until the vat was considered full enough, after which a fire was started under it to start the sugar water boiling, and took close watch after it commenced to boil. Seems to me they took some home for mother to finish after it had thickened enough to carry it across the river in a boat. No fording with a team as the river was still too high after the ice had gone out.

A shelter had been built of rough lumber, shanty style, to protect one from inclement weather and to furnish sleeping quarters etc. during the sugar making season for those having to remain at night. In this shanty were an improvised bed, a table, a chair, and a long bench which came in very handy for placing receptacles in which to pour the warm sugar to harden when it was finished, "sugaring off" as it was called. Father slept here at night during the sugar making, going home in the evening with Will to get a warm supper and assist with the chores, returning again to the camp while Will remained over night to do the chores next morning after which he too returned to the camp taking food sufficient for the day and a warm breakfast for father who met him on the shore with a boat.

Two or three times I had been allowed to accompany Will on his return to camp, to spend the day following father around and witnessing these operations, otherwise I could not relate to them. At this time I had not started to school, and this was my only chance to witness sugar making. When the time came for "sugaring off" every receptacle one could muster together was collected and put in use.

All pans, basins, cake tins, etc. were filled with the warm sugar, and then the long bench and table in the shanty were brought out into the open where it would cool more quickly and solidify; then it was packed into a washtub and taken to the boat when ready to leave at night. Father returning to look after the fire and gathering the sugar water still running, all of which must be looked after. This was his nightly vigil until the season was over. Alone with his gun for protection, he needed it during this "Robinson Crusoe" existence. But all things have an end and the sugar making soon was finished and the work of preparing the ground for the season's crops was commenced, which took much time and labor to accomplish.

CHAPTER 21

Prairie Chickens

PRAIRIE CHICKENS, NOW ALMOST EXTINCT in these parts were found in large numbers in the tall prairie grass, their natural habitation. I remember of one time while following father around as I often did, in crossing the prairie on foot, a mother hen flew up from her nest at our approach and it seemed to me I never saw so many eggs in one nest before. Father put his hand out at our approach and said "now don't touch them, they will not hatch if they are handled." Allowing me to have a good look he said "We had better go on so the mother hen can return to her nest before the eggs are cold." I never forgot that prairie chicken's nest full of dainty eggs. What a wonderful sight that would be today and I am hopeful there may be some way to protect these dainty birds from extinction before the last one becomes the victim of some hunter's gun.

During the month of November this same year, 1859, father had returned from a trip to town, the girls seeing him in the act of loosening the horses from the wagon hurried out with myself closely following, and asked as usual "any mail or news?" Father was looking very sober, rather downcast as he answered "No mail today; but the news is they have hung John Brown!" Then shaking his head in a despondent manner he said "I fear it means war" and his fears were realized within the following eighteen months, Fort Sumter was fired upon and the War Between the States was on with all its tragic events of more than four years

CHAPTER 22

Revenge is Sweet

ONE EVENING DURING OUR LAST summer on this farm father was returning from the barn which was across the road from the house at that time; he saw an Indian leading his pony, while he seemed to be looking for something. Father coming upon him suddenly, asked after the usual greeting, what he was looking for. The Indian answered in the usual way, and said in his best English "looking for tracks" - trying to find some of his tribe he had become separated from. Father told him that a band of Indians had passed through that morning, stopping for a short time and then had crossed the river into the big timber where he thought they were camping. On receiving this information the Indian gave a leap into the air that for high jumping certainly would have won him a first prize, and let out a whoop that carried far across the river into the timber. Immediately a faint answer came back and he was satisfied that he had found his tribe. Father said to him "the river is high and it is now dark, perhaps you had better not try crossing tonight but wait for daylight to swim your pony across. I will feed it and give you something to eat and a place to sleep and in the morning you can safely cross". The Indian readily accepted the favor. The pony was fed and watered and the Indian accompanied father to the house where Mother was informed of the circumstances. She immediately prepared something for him to eat as he tearfully was telling father his troubles. To what tribe he belonged I do not know, but the Sac, Fox, Sioux and some other tribes seemed to be in constant warfare with each other. Murder, pillage and kidnapping seemed to be their mode of warfare.

He wept while relating to father that his parents and others of his family had been murdered, and his squaw and papoose had been carried away captives by the enemy, while he and others of his tribe were absent on a hunt. He was well armed, with gun, tomahawk and a large murderous looking knife.

But he said "Me no kill white man, me kill no white squaw, me kill no papoose, me kill big Injun!" flourishing his knife as though the enemy were present. Father told him that a few days earlier a tribe of Indians had passed through, stopping as was their custom, asking for food etc., and in the lead was a very handsome looking young squaw with a papoose, carried in the usual way on her back. Instead of riding alone as customary, an Indian brave was riding by her side as though for protection, while the others were following in the usual manner - one behind the other. She was very handsome and well dressed in her Indian garb of buckskin with fringe and beads, and her clothing looked unusually fresh and clean. This tribe did not tarry long but moved on as though in a hurry. On being told of this the Indian was sure it was the tribe he was after. He seemed heartbroken. Revenge and the rescue of his squaw and papoose was his one desire. When the time came to retire he rolled up in his blanket and laid on the floor instead of occupying the bed on the lounge which mother had prepared for him.

The sight of that murderous looking knife he had flourished around unnerved Hala, and she feared to go upstairs to bed without first hiding all sharp knives. Being persuaded that it would be unnecessary she was glad next morning that she had not done so. When she and Margaret came downstairs they saw him sitting by the kitchen stove using that much feared knife to punch tobacco down into his pipe.

After having breakfast and his pony fed and watered he departed to join his friends in waiting across the river. He had gained some useful knowledge to aid him in his pursuit of the perpetrators of this atrocious deed. Expressing his thanks as best he could for all favors extended him he departed on his mission.

CHAPTER 23

Fishing and Hunting Grounds

THIS SAME FALL ON MR. Perry's return from the west, we moved back to our home in the Freeman log store building which was on the main traveled road. The frequent visits of Indians continued, always begging for food.

A favorite rendezvous for them was Mason's Grove (Mason City) where they found excellent hunting especially in the heavy timbered country around Clear Lake, in which fishing was excellent. It was an ideal place for their needs.

Of the many tribes frequenting these places, it seems the Winnebago's must have been denied that privilege for some reason. At one time while up there on a hunting expedition their village of tepees was attacked during the absence of the braves and many of their women and children were murdered. During the fight the squaws did their best in their own defense as many of the attackers paid them penalty with their lives. The ground was strewn with the dead. One Winnebago boy of sixteen shot down one of the enemy and was himself killed. Being decapitated, his head was carried off and his body lying where he fell. The attackers scalped their victims and carried off their own dead. This ghastly sight confronted the Winnebago's on their return. It looked as though it was done to discourage any attempt to again enter this territory. Is it to be on the bank of the Cedar River where they could fish and hunt unmolested? Their village on the south side of Freeman had been their home before the advent of any white man. There was no evidence of having been trouble by other tribes as long as they kept away from Clear Lake and its surrounding territory.

After the land had been bought by the government, it seemed they could not resist the longing for this former home and they kept returning to their old haunts for many years. The Cedar River though abundantly supplied with fish could not be compared to Clear Lake with it broad expanse of water and the heavy timber which surrounded it at that time. But here they were at peace with plenty of good fishing and hunting. There was no evidence of any battles having been fought in this vicinity. Not until 1862 did the Winnebago's cease coming.

CHAPTER 24

Seeing My First Black Man

IN 1860 FATHER TOOK ME with him on one of his trips to Cedar Falls. Mother packed my best clothes in a satchel, and my hat which could not be packed was tied to one of the bows of the wagon cover. I had on my everyday clothes with a sunbonnet on my head. Of course, all was fresh and clean.

At that time it took three days with good luck to make the trip and return. Paved roads were unknown, in fact unheard of. Toward evening we came to a grove and stopped for the night. Father built a camp fire to cook our supper. There was food in the provision box and one of Mother's apple pies. Father heated water to make coffee which he liked with his food. In the clearing a few rods distant there was a large log house with other buildings, a thrifty looking farm for that early day. Father said he knew the people and they were very nice. I was glad someone was nearby. As darkness came on, the howling of wolves gave me a creepy feeling, though I had heard them every night at home. But in a strange place it was scarier, and I snuggled close to Father and felt safe.

Early next morning after breakfast we continued the drive to Cedar Falls. On nearing town Father drove to one side of the road to clean me up and change my clothes. He had water in a large jug, a wash basin, bath cloth, castile soap, towels, hair brush and comb. After giving me a thorough scrubbing he put on my clean underclothes, my best stockings and shoes, my best dress, combed my hair and lastly my hat was taken from the wagon bow, placed on my head and the ribbons tied under my chin. He surveyed me with a satisfied look and continued into town. Arriving there we went into a store where he made purchases. We went outside and he sat me on a large dry goods box and said: "I have some business to attend to at the depot before we leave. You can sit here in the shade and watch the people passing back and forth on the street." I was satisfied to remain where I was having no desire to go to the depot in the hot sun.

Many people were passing, among them ladies with straw bonnets, ribbon and flower trimmed, carrying dainty parasols affording them little protection from the sun. Their voluminous dress skirts were held out with large hoop-skirts giving people little chance to get by. I had a real fancy for hoopskirts myself and did not criticize even it did crowd people off the sidewalk.

While in the midst of these interesting sights a colored man came by. Never having seen a colored person I was frightened nearly to death. Oh! But he was black! My heart stood still for a second. It must have missed a beat. He was well dressed and walked along with an easy satisfied air. People who met him greeted him smilingly, relieving me of my fears. I thought he couldn't be dangerous or people would not be so friendly. He was very straight showing no signs of toil. If he had ever been in bondage it must have been as a valet to his master who had given him his freedom for some reason.

Later on Father returned and greeting me smilingly asked if I had enjoyed the sights. I did not tell him of the fright I had during his absence. I was not harmed and did not complain and told him I enjoyed the sights very much. He replied that we had better start back now, as it had been a long time since breakfast. "We will stop in the grove where we spend last night and I will cook our supper. The water is good and I'll boil some potatoes and fry some salt pork, and make gravy. I will try to remember to salt it…" He had cooked a chicken on the way and we couldn't eat it, so it was given to the neighbors' dog. He didn't seem to mind it by the way he went after it. This was embarrassing to Father who was quite a good cook. We had company for supper that night. He was a man who had no cover on his wagon using a tarpaulin to protect his goods. Father had invited him to sleep in our wagon and have supper with us. I thought the unsalted chicken was a great joke on Father. The loss of the chicken had been a disappointment to me as well as to Father.

The next morning after breakfast we started on. Father had bought something in dress goods for each one and they would be pleased. As always, Mother got the "lion's share." Hers was more expensive. Mother was a queen in Father's eyes. He had excellent taste in dress goods and he always bought the best, seeming to know what was most becoming to each one.

The family was watching for us when we arrived. During the first few days I was the center of attraction. And though I had been gone but three days it seemed like a week to me. It had been my first trip away from home without Mother, and to me it was quite a venture.

Mother always took her children with her when she went to spend an afternoon or all day with a friend. All mothers did the same in the long ago. And it was a happy time for the children on those occasions.

CHAPTER 25

A Sleigh Ride to Church

IN THE EARLY DAYS PEOPLE seemed to appreciate the chance to hear a gospel sermon and would go many miles in the most severe winter weather to listen to one of the itinerant ministers traveling through the country on horseback in the Master's service.

Word had come that a meeting was to be held in the home of Mr. J.M. Howard in what is now Riverton Twisp, six or eight miles south of St. Charles. What denomination he represented made no difference. It meant a sermon was to be preached and Father and Mother decided to attend. The weather was quite severe, the snow deep, roads poor and the trip must be made by driving down the river on the ice which was perfectly safe at this time.

The night of the meeting arrived and all of us were in readiness. Father had placed straw in the sleigh box spreading blankets thereon for the family to sit on covering our heads with quilts to keep out the cold. We were all cozy and warm for the drive while the music of jingling sleigh bells sounded very cheerful and deadened the sound of the squeaking sleigh runners over the snow.

On arriving we found all rooms filled with eager listeners. The text of the sermon I do not remember, being very young, but remember one of the hymns they sang: "Am I a soldier of the Cross? A Follower of the Lamb?" etc. This hymn was familiar to us and seemed to be a favorite of Father and one he always sang or tried to sing while rocking the baby to sleep for Mother who was always busy. This being his nightly job when at home, and whether he could carry a tune or not it had a soothing effect on the baby and soon he was free to resume his reading.

The sermon which had seemed of interest to all brought to a close with the singing of another of those old time hymns and followed by an earnest benediction by the minister. All were appreciative of the sermon and clasped the hand of the speaker in brotherly greeting, while thanking him for coming to them with his message of salvation for all who were a thirst for its promises.

On returning home the fire which Father had banked as usual had failed to keep, with not a spark remaining. Taking the tongs he hurried to our nearest neighbor and soon returned holding a fire brand with the tongs. Soon a bright fire was snapping and cracking in the heating stove. Plenty of kindling had been prepared before leaving for the meeting and no one was chilled while waiting for the fire to burn. Little waste paper there was to help in starting a fire, only two newspapers, the New York Tribune and our local paper, the Republican Intelligencer, were preserved each week with no thought of using them for kindling fires. Later on Mother used them to paper the log wall in lieu of wall paper. While not so attractive, it gave the walls a clean look. This primitive living may seem crude to many, but people were happy and content. In a new country people were more interested in each other, sharing their joys and sorrows and the ties of friendship seemed much stronger than they do now.

CHAPTER 26

Waverly Hill, Strawberries and Snakes

From what we now call "Waverly Hill," a name given it when the Illinois Central Railroad had reached Waverly bringing the outside world closer to us with the telegraph, etc., we had sighted the stage coming twice a week with passengers and mail. We had watched the many different tribes of Indians so long as they continued passing through until the last uprising in 1862 when they were no longer seen.

Later, from that hill top, our boys when starting for the seat of war, had their last glimpse of home, waving goodbye as they passed out of sight, some never to return. The hill will always mean much to us, changed though it be, bringing memories both pleasant and sad.

It was up that hill many of us had winded our way in search of the luscious wild strawberries we knew would be there on the exact spot where now stands the early home of C.G. Patten, Sr. And how shocked we were when we saw our precious strawberry patch had been plowed up! The purpose we did not know.

One particular time as several of us were searching, I noticed in the grass by the roadside, a snake strange to me with such a beautiful shape and coloring, light blue. It was traveling along close to me, close enough to touch it. An older girl exclaimed: "Oh! There is a blue racer!" With a stick she started in but I was glad to see it making good headway through the grass in another direction. She failed in her purpose for which I was thankful. I enjoyed studying that snake, strange to me, never having seen one like it before, nor have I since. It showed no disposition to fight traveling along like a pet dog.

I would here mention another snake which I saw many years later, the only specimen of its kind I ever saw. I needed no one to give me information as it let me know without doubt, what it was. We were living about two blocks east of the Andre Brewery (now only a memory), when one warm day our eldest boy then about three years old, had climbed on the board fence enclosing the place and called out, "Oh, look at the big worm!" We went out immediately and there coiled up by the roadside was a very large snake that rose up, neck swelling out to a large proportion and emitting a whistling sound. It was a "blow snake!" Finding a weapon, we called to some boys herding cows nearby and with their help we soon dispatched it, though not without a strong fight on its part. It had offered the challenge and was going to die fighting. What we would have done without the help of those boys we do not know. Glad I was when they triumphantly carried it away from our sight and proud they were with their trophy.

Now back to the hill once more. In the beginning it was a broad expanse of unbroken prairie, brilliant with wild flowers beginning to bloom early in the spring and lasting until late in the fall, each kind in their season. There was not a tree or bush on the site of this hill but being covered thickly with native prairie grass. All the present trees have grown up in the places where rocks were quarried in 1870 and on for some years. In the fall of 1862 this hill was the scene of an early day prairie fire starting at night. It was a thrilling sight to all those witnessing it. Knowing the outcome of those fires when once they were out of control, it struck terror to the hearts of all on-lookers. The few buildings on the south side of the river were saved.

This was an eventful month, October 1862; the business section of St. Charles was wiped out by fire starting at the Kelly Hotel, spreading to all nearby buildings. The Magnolia Hotel standing on the corner now occupied by the May Drug Company was entirely consumed together with all stores, dry good, grocery and the only hardware called the Tin Shop operated and owned by Carl Merchel Sr. He was the father of Mrs. Theresa Hausberg, who manufactured his tin ware in the early days as did all tinsmiths. We often think of it now, handmade and of the best quality.

Heroic efforts were used in saving the Intelligencer building on the corner north of the Magnolia Hotel. For a wonder it was saved with the meager facilities then at hand. People were carrying water in wooden pails, from the few wells nearby and from the river. It is one of the few landmarks of old St. Charles left standing, though not in the same spot where it was built. It was of great importance in the building of our present Charles City.

Mr. Hildreth carried on his back, from the sawmill near the river, much of the lumber which went into the building. It was good and heavy native oak. He put his shoulder to the wheel and with determination won over all obstacles with which the early pioneers had to contend. His was an example it would be well for all young men to follow; he never shirked when confronted with hard work.

CHAPTER 27

4th of July

Mrs. Mary E. Leaman, 1308 East Clark Street, has written an interesting account of a Fourth of July celebration in 1861, eighty years ago, from memory. She states that the southwest side of the river here, at that time, was quite heavily timbered and the men in charge of the celebration had had all the brush and some smaller trees removed to make room for the speaker's stand, seats for the listeners and two or three long tables for the free dinner served by the ladies.

The account of the 1861 celebration follows:

When we celebrated our country's Independence in the good old-fashioned way on July 4th, people were awakened at 4:00 in the morning from their slumbers by the firing of the homemade cannon and anvils in the blacksmith shops. Boys and girls hurriedly dressed themselves and soon were outside with harmless firecrackers to begin this day of days. In the morning breeze, martial music, the drum and fife would be heard and the celebrating of this all important day, our nations independence was beginning in true patriotic style; a day of thrills for everyone, especially the children.

The officers of the day on their fiery steeds with their gay trappings were to me a grand and thrilling sight. They had over one shoulder a broad band of bright red cloth looped on the opposite side and on each end was a tassel of the same color. These uniforms in our eyes were beautiful.

On the south side of the river a stand had been erected in the grove for speakers and singers, long benches of plank provided seats for the listeners, and two long tables built by driving stakes in the ground and covering the tops with planks. These were ready for the picnic dinner which would follow the exercises, consisting of speeches, singing and the reading of the

Declaration of Independence with more or less flag waving and cheering during the speaking.

Quite early in the morning farm wagons began arriving with families and friends with their large baskets of food to place on the table. Such wonderful food they brought in those baskets! Roast beef, roast pork, roast chicken with all the trimmings of pies and cakes. What did they not have? One thrifty housewife placed on one of the tables a roast pig browned to a finish with a bunch of parsley in its mouth. As I remember it now it may have weighed close to twenty five pounds. I wondered what she had roasted it in. It was such a beautiful brown.

At 9:30 a parade by the "Ragamuffins" as they were called, and I think the name was very appropriate, the rag part of their name fitted them perfectly. Some of them looked like rag tramps and some of the hideous false faces were really very frightful for small children. They did not realize this was merely a comic parade of men and boys they most all knew. They carried tiny horns and whistles which they blew while on the march, making all the noise possible. This was the time to serve the tempting dinner the ladies had in readiness to which all did justice. The children were served after the adults had eaten, and plenty of nice food there was for them being waited on faithfully by the ladies. A feeling of sadness comes over me as I remember that none of these ladies, who so kindly waited on us children on that day are no longer with us, all have passed to the great beyond. In memory, I see their smiling faces as they flitted about serving each of us.

At 2:30 the crowd crossed the river and assembled in the public square, as it was called, to witness further exercises consisting of foot races, sack races, climbing the greased pole, catching the greased pig and also wrestling matches. Prizes were given each winner. Those competing in the sack race were placed in a strong gunny sack with nothing outside except their head, their legs and arms being imprisoned with the sack. This was a difficult feat with many a tumble during this performance and much loud cheering by the spectators. I think they earned their money doing this stunt.

All were cash prizes except the greased pig. Catching it was their prize as the pig was good pay for the winner. This was not so easily done as one might think. At last it was captured, but how one held on to the greasy thing is a mystery to me. This closed the exercises for the day. At night fireworks on a small scale, it would seem to us today, were witnessed by an appreciative crowd. No accidents happened to mar the pleasures of the day. Then this glorious 4th of July celebration passes into history in the memory of those present.

I do not remember of seeing one intoxicated person that day, although we had open saloons. I think perhaps that free dinner served by the ladies had saved them. What may have happened later at night, I cannot say.

Before closing this narrative I will tell of an incident which happened early in the day. A young man riding on horseback stopped his horse at the river bank, dismounted and tied it to a small tree and left to join the crowd. Soon after, three or four young men, mischief bent, tied a bunch of firecrackers on the end of the horse's tail and set them off. The terrified horse's heels went into the air as he plunged around, the crackers continuing to snap and crack until the last one had burned out. The horse must have been newly shod by the way his shoes glittered in the sunlight as his heels went up. We scampered to get out of the way of danger; I and a girl friend who had witnessed this while those mischievous young men were convulsed with laughter over their prank. They certainly will remember this if still living, which I doubt, as I was a small girl at the time, and they were grownup men.

The Star Spangled Banner was always sung on these occasions. This time it was sung by Miss Lucy Bliss, one of the early school teachers. She was a fine singer, ever ready to serve the public on such occasions. In memory I hear her voice as it rang out strong and clear in the open air and with such patriotic fervor as she sang. It could not fail to imbue her listeners with a strong feeling of patriotism. Like the Goddess of Liberty she stood there holding in her hands the stars and stripes waving them gently as she sang.

CHAPTER 28

Doing Mother's "Calling"

A Sunday school convention was being held in the new Floyd County Courthouse. Although a church had been built it would not seat so large a crowd. All large gatherings were held in the Courthouse. Delegates from the Sunday Schools of all the nearby towns and surrounding country were supposed to be in attendance. Our friend, Mary Eliza, was left at our house by her family that we might go together as we loved to do. With such a short distance to go we were perfectly safe without an escort.

It had happened that we had been given the same name of Mary. Father for some reason always called me "Molly" and by that name I was known to my schoolmates and friends. Being Molly and Mary was less confusing to others as we always sat together and studied our lessons from the same books. Who ever got the new book first would share it with the other. We were very happy as we started out hand in hand for the courthouse, dressed in our best clothes of which I think we both were conscious of. The meeting had seemed very short to us so under the circumstances and on being dismissed there was no alternative for us but to follow the crowd. We went slowly and soberly from the spiral stairway, always a great pleasure to us heretofore and thought of going home. We would remove our finery to be replaced by our everyday clothes and this seemed dismal to us. What could we do to prolong the time of remaining "dressed up?" We halted to discuss the matter before leaving the yard when a happy thought came to us. Why not make some calls on some of the ladies who had called on our mothers? That's what we decided to do. We would cross the new foot bridge all by ourselves. The bridge had a railing and we could not fall into the river. That matter settled, we wondered who to call on. We decided it should be Mrs. Hildreth, the editor's wife. They lived on Main Street close to the printing office. They had a doorbell which would be a great pleasure to ring, adding dignity to the call. Who would ring the bell?

Mary, being taller, would more easily reach the handle and give it a turn (no electric bells were in existence those days).

The bell was answered almost immediately by Mrs. Hildreth, who smilingly received us and ushered us into her parlor with its nice horse hair upholstered furniture and bright carpet (ours was rag). My eyes took this in at a glance. Introductions were not necessary, Mrs. Hildreth, knowing who her callers were seemed very pleased. Amused perhaps at the effort we had made to assume the airs of grownups and trying to appear very dignified. By her tactfulness she helped us to become our real selves, saving us any further strain of acting. She began by showing us the dolls, books and playthings which had belonged to her own little Mary of whom death had robbed her a few years previous. She told of little incidents occurring during her short life and soon we began to feel our real selves. I think it afforded our hostess more real pleasure. Mrs. Hildreth was a lover of children, especially girls. She was a beautiful character of a woman.

Time flew by swiftly with her mode of entertainment and we had forgotten all about the other calls we had planned to make until she arose from her chair and going to a book case returned with the stereoscope and a bunch of views which she placed on the table near us and said it was time for her to begin preparing tea. She wished us to remain and have it with her. "It would be a great pleasure to have you and while I am busy you will find these views very interesting" she said. Recovering from the shock of realizing we had stayed all this time at one place and forgetting about our other calls we had a doubt about the propriety of remaining to tea and wondered what Mother would think. This gave me some uneasiness. But Mrs. Hildreth had given us little chance to refuse her hospitality going immediately into the kitchen as though the matter was settled. We were having such a delightful time we resigned ourselves to the afterthought of whatever might occur. Mother had her own ideas about any infraction of her rules, namely going places without permission. Plenty of hazel brush was nearby and I knew the sting of those keen little switches. Mother felt she must know where her children were.

We busied ourselves looking at the views which we greatly enjoyed taking our turn through the stereoscope. Before we realized there had been time,

Mrs. Hildreth returned to the room and announced that tea was ready. She ushered us into the dining room, seating us at the table where we were facing the door through which Mr. Hildreth came in from his office followed by the boys in his employ. As was customary in those days, so much was paid a year to the apprentices with board and washing. The fabulous sum of $25.00 for the first year, $50 for the second year, $75 for the third year, and $100 for the fourth year.

My brother, Will, among the other boys, looked his surprise on seeing his little sister Mollie and her friend Mary seated at the table. He had little sister Mollie and her friend Mary seated at the table. He had not been informed there was to be company for tea that night. Mrs. Hildreth raised her hand as the boys came in and said, "Boys, you see I have guests for tea tonight and wish you to be on your best behavior." They bowed and seated themselves like gentlemen should, with no further evidence of surprise.

I always will remember that menu. Everything looked so inviting. The meat was salt pork, properly fried. In those days there were no meat markets to carry fresh meat. Of course when there was company, the potatoes were mashed with plenty of butter dotting the top; and rice, of which I was very fond and cooked just like Mother always cooked hers; hot soda biscuits with plenty of fresh butter, honey and real maple syrup. There was also the usual supply of jelly, pickles and cheese. Dessert consisted of a very nice looking cake of which I did not partake, not being fond of sweets. But what interested me the most was a large glass bowl full of red currants covered with white sugar which looked like frost was on them. Being more fond of anything sour than I was of sweets I looked with approval on this part of the menu. Very few of the early settlers possessed the tame currants, so common with us today, unless they were wise to bring some roots along with them when they migrated to this new state. People must depend upon the wild fruit to supply their tables; the timber was full of it, free for the taking, but the tame ones served by our hostess were a real delicacy.

Our nice meal finished, so thoroughly enjoyed, we were compelled by the lateness to break the rule of etiquette and adopt that of beggars, to 'eat and run.' We hated to do this but think our hostess understood the situation when we announced that we must be going. We thanked her for our entertainment and left. I knew I would be asked by Mother if we had. She would be shocked by my confession that we had gone calling and remained for tea.

We started home with some uncertainty in our minds as to the outcome of our escapade. But one comforting thought was mine, we could cross that bridge again and had a delightful time, and if I got a switching it was well worth it. With those comforting thoughts I hurried home listening to the gurgling water with no fear of falling in the river. Mary didn't stop to hear my confession or the sentence pronounced on me. It was late and she hurried home to her sister Anna who had taken the place of her mother since her passing. "Child alive!" Where on earth have you been? I have been worried to death!" Mother exclaimed. Then I began explaining to her that the meeting was so short we thought we might make a few calls while we were dressed up. "I knew you owed some calls and I thought I might pay them for you. You know you never seem to find time. But we made one call because we stayed too long at Mrs. Hildreth's place. She was glad we came, I know. She showed us little Mary's dolls and playthings and told us of many things about her. And then she gave us a stereoscope with a bunch of nice views to look at. When she said she must be preparing tea, we could look at them, and she wished us to remain and have tea with her. I was scared when I found it was so late. She didn't give us a chance to refuse for she went right out of the room and shut the door. I wish we had a stereoscope and some views!"

For the time being in my enthusiasm, I had forgotten that I was on trial for a transgression so I continued on, telling all that happened. Mother while she looked severe had become an interested listener. She appreciated my thought of trying to help out in her social obligations and realized I had meant well, so she changed her mind as to any merited punishment. Had I for my own amusement gone to play with some children, perhaps soiling or tearing my clothes, it would have been a different matter. Circumstances alter cases and Mother excused me this time telling me not to go places again without permission, as it caused her too much worry.

CHAPTER 29

First Kerosene Lamp

FATHER RETURNED FROM ONE OF his trips to Cedar Falls, bringing the first kerosene lamp we had ever seen. He called it a "fluid lamp." Candles had been the only lights of all public buildings and homes heretofore. This beer-mug-shaped lamp was quite an improvement in the way of light. The burner consisted of two funnel-shaped pipes in the center, through which two round wicks extended into the oil. The lamp had no chimney and these two round wicks furnished a light somewhat brighter than that of two candles. This caused much excitement among the few neighbors who gathered to see this wonderful light. Soon lamps having chimneys were in general used by all, though still using candle to move from room to room.

This lamp and mother's candle molds, both cherished mementos of early days, were destroyed when the Cleveland house, father's first hotel, was burned in 1878. The fire started in the night, and had gotten beyond control when it was discovered. The guests and all fled in their night clothes. With no organized fire company, and no water system it made firefighting slow and difficult, especially when well started, it meant total destruction of any building.

I'll tell about that fire now. Sister Agnes ran down the street ringing a bell and shouting fire, trying to rouse the inhabitants. Soon a large crowd gathered at the scene. A few things from the first floor were carried outside. But the second floor containing the bookcase and old family pictures of the daguerreotype style end cases (impossible to replace) was consumed. Nothing on that floor was saved; it was a seething mass of flames. So different from now, when there are telephones and chemicals at hand! It had started in the attic where much unused clothing hung from the rafters. Candles were carried about, being handier than a lamp and it was thought that some of the help going up there to look for something might have held a candle too high. This would ignite some of the clothing. Mother, with others of the family, fled in her night clothes, barefoot. We were taken into the homes of near neighbors, who by this time had been aroused from their slumbers.

This building was afterward replaced by one closer in a more desired building for a hotel. Father continued to landlord until failing health necessitated his retirement. This last hotel was known as the Leonard house. But on retiring, Father asked that the name be no longer used and had it painted over, leaving to his successor the choosing of a name. For some years it was known as the Brainard House. The property was afterward sold, the building torn down, and the ground used for other purposes.

In the early autumn of 1863 the large log house east of the Freeman store, the Samuel Hackley, Sr. House was burned down. Nothing was saved and we lost our nearest neighbor. This was one of the first pioneer homes.

Friends from the north side of the river, seeing the fire came immediately, taking the family home with them until a second house could be secured, which happened to be on the north side. A picture of this home drawn by Ezra Lamborn, Mrs. Hackley's eldest son, a boy of 12 years, was a perfect replica of this house. In it we had attended our Sunday school in Freeman with Rev. Windsor (congregational) an early minister holding services, regardless of denomination. This was before a church was built and in this house also was held the first school on the south side, in the winter of 1858-1859. The home of H. Merten stands on this ground, occupying almost the same spot.

CHAPTER 30

Fleeing From the Indians

An unusual noise at the door one night which father answered and on opening it there stood an elderly woman, possibly in her sixties, a pack on her back so large it hindered her entrance through the door upon being invited in. Father had to assist her. When inside this pack proved to be a featherbed, well roped and fastened to her back. She was crying and in her broken language - being a foreigner - tried to make her wants know. "Vataloo-stach," meaning "stage" they soon learned. After trying numberless times to understand all she had tried so hard to tell them, learned she was among those who had been the victims of an attack by Indians; her family all having been killed, while she managed to escape with her featherbed, hiding in the tall grass. Hiding in daylight, traveling by night, living on wild plums, grapes, etc. so plentiful there, she was trying to reach Waterloo where she had friends. She was a pitiful sight, her heavy leather shoes were completely worn out, no longer protected her feet, which were bleeding from contact with thorns etc.

Mother prepared a warm supper for her, a good bed on which to rest her weary body and father told her he would go over the river and see what he could do toward getting transportation for her by stage next morning. He saw some of the businessmen, related to them her situation and they readily responded by contributing money enough to pay her fare and something besides to supply her needs until she could find her friends. Was she happy? You should have seen her! She went to each of her benefactors, and clasping the hands of each in her own, kissed them while raining tears of gratitude upon them.

When the stage arrived next morning father accompanied her out and had some difficulty in making her understand that she could not take her featherbed inside the stage, but that it must be put on top where all baggage was placed. He finally made her understand there would be no room for other passengers, besides it was too large to get it through the stage door and she had to part with her precious load until they arrived at Waterloo. At last she was comfortably seated in the stage and smiling through her tears as the driver cracked his whip over the backs of the four horse team and she was on her way to "V-a-t-e-r-l-o-o."

Immediately following this occurrence was the arrival of a family one day in an emigrant wagon; having with them a boy ten years of age, whom they had overtaken on the road while they were in flight from an attack by Indians, and learned that he too had fled for the same reason and was the only member of his family left alive.

His story was that he had been sent to drive the cattle home from their grazing ground some distance away and while going through the timber to reach them he had heard screaming and shooting of guns. Not knowing what it meant, he continued on, gathering the cattle together and started them toward home. On emerging from the timber he saw laying around the yard the bodies of his parents and all the family. Each one had been scalped and their bodies stripped of most of the clothing they had on. He alone had escaped, being on his mission of getting the cattle.

He fled back into the timber from this awful sight confronting him, trying to get away unseen from the murderous savages. He continued on through the timber knowing he would be more hidden traveling in a southerly direction as nearly as he could discern, for some days. His only sustenance had been wild plums, crabapples and grapes which he found on his journey through the timber and he was badly in need of food.

Emerging into the open country, when he thought it might be safe to do so, he found a traveled road where he was overtaken by this family who on hearing his story took him in with them. He told them he had relatives in Waterloo, Iowa, the only ones he knew of and was hoping he might find them. This family having no certain destination in view; their only object being to put as many miles between themselves and danger as possible, thought to take him to his friends. All inhabitants here were living in terror and they did not tarry long after getting something to eat but continued on their way. Mother, it seemed, was often cooking a meal and making beds on the floor, if it happened to be at night, for the many people in their flight.

Many emigrants passing through when overtaken by darkness and fearing to cross the river at night would stop and asked for food and shelter until daylight. This was an added hardship for mother but she never refused them and would set herself about preparing a meal for them and would do so willingly. Sometimes there would be a number of children in the family to cook for, but people provided their own bedding which they spread on the floor on retiring. Mother was patient and kindly through it all, remembering what it meant to a tired mother with little ones after a hard day of traveling.

These were two of the happenings during the Indian outbreak of 1862, while memories of the massacre of people at Spirit Lake and Okoboji in February 1857, and were still fresh in the mind of everyone. The Indians in Minnesota, being dissatisfied with their home there and being influenced by the Sioux became troublesome. Even the Winnebago Indians, feeling sore over the loss of the home land they had loved, although it had been bought from them by the Government, they were homesick, and not having yet received all their pay and being in sore need of food, etc. enduring much suffering from privation and sickness were on the verge of joining in with their enemies, the Sioux, against the whites. But that was averted and they soon gave up all thought of turning against their former friends and were given a change, being sent west.

'Tis hard to realize how these things could have happened in this peaceful and prosperous community; but these are true happenings, with no exaggeration. The Freeman log store, our early home, was on a direct route and we were visited by many in their flight as well as by those seeking new homes in the North and West.

CHAPTER 31

Indian Scare of 1862

DURING THE UPRISING IN MINNESOTA among the Indians, where so many white people were killed, many of the inhabitants here had made preparation to flee from their home at a moment's warning. Covers were placed on their wagons; bedding, clothing and cooking utensils were placed therein, and in some instances horses would be completely harnessed ready to hook on to the wagon at the first alarm sounded.

Mother was very much frightened on being left at home with her children while father made "just one more trip" to Cedar Falls. Arrangements had been made to place the women and children in the court room on the second floor of the Court House, while the men left at home could guard it against an attack should the Indians come; arms and ammunition having been placed there in readiness. Father said to mother "Scouts are out, and if there is any immediate danger you will be warned. Take the children and go to the Court House; there you will be just as safe as if I was with you."

For three nights we were put to bed with our clothes on, even our shoes and stockings. Mother sat up to insure against missing the call. And we remember on awakening in the night of seeing her by the dim light of a tallow candle standing in the middle of the floor in a listening attitude, hands clasped and a look of fear on her face.

During these experiences our cousin, Hala, whose home was with us until marriage was teaching school twelve miles south of town. She had walked most of that distance to reach home; her school having been closed because of the Indian scare. She had started out amidst the pleadings of the family with whom she was boarding as they feared for her to undertake it. She arrived home unharmed while we were in the midst of our fright. Happily just then word came that a detachment of soldiers had been sent and the Indians were driven back into Minnesota, and a number of the Sioux were afterward hanged.

At the time of this Indian scare of 1862, heavy timber was between our house and the Court House, no streets being laid out. A narrow road, leading from the river road over the court house hill - a steep one then - and at the right as you neared the top of the hill, were a number of graves, early burials, mostly children, I think, and not far from the two log houses having been occupied by the Milo Gilbert and Wyatt families, some of whose children had been buried there. One roof covered both these houses, with an alley of a few feet between, and a door leading into each one, small windows, placed high up, presumably to prevent prowling Indians from peering in, pressing their noses against the window panes as was their habit, frightening the inmates who would be easy targets for those with evil designs. These houses stood a little to the northeast of where the Lutheran Church stands, on what is now East Gilbert Street. A large Burr-Oak tree at the south end of the little park, near the oil station is near the site of those two frontier homes. How that noble monarch of the forest ever escaped the ax of some thoughtless person is a mystery. 'Tis one of the few left which links the past with the present. The tree had escaped the woodman's ax and was still standing the last time we were in the vicinity. We always looked for it, though many years had passed. In memory we see it all, just as it looked, in the summer of 1857. We are glad to have been here before the beauty of nature had been destroyed.

CHAPTER 32

Floyd County's First Courthouse

THE FIRST COURT HOUSE, a stone one, was at last finished, in May, 1861, after much wrangling and bitterness over the location of the county seat, and shortly after the firing on Fort Sumter and the Civil war between the North and South was on, with all the heartbreaks it brought to so many mothers, wives and sweethearts.

Public meetings were held in the court room of the Court House when the call for volunteers came, asking a quota of 75,000 of Iowa's men in this first call, meaning a great depletion of the able bodied men and boys so much needed at home. But no faltering was there; loyal hearts beat in the breasts of Iowa's men and boys, and a ready response was theirs, far in excess of the number called for. But not to the men alone is credit due, as these mothers and wives were left to carry on the work of the absent ones, tilling the soil to raise the needed food for home consumption and for the soldier boys at the front; and wielding the ax for fuel, as with heavy hearts they anxiously awaited news of their loved ones.

Busy women they were; no time for powder and paint had they. The hum of the spinning wheel and the clicking of knitting needles was a familiar sound in every household. So much of their work, knitting, sewing etc. was done at night, by the dim light of tallow candles, the daylight being used for the outside work formerly done by the men and boys.

The fife and drum was the music which had accompanied our boys when they started for the war, following them through all the hard-fought battles where the lives of so many were sacrificed.

No sorrow had come to our family by death while residing in our frontier home, but with the advent of the Civil War much sorrow came to father and mother, and those of us who were old enough to realize what it all meant, and many dark days followed.

First came a division in mother's family, causing her to shed many tears. Both father and her were born and reared near the Kentucky line but father was a strong abolitionist and she took her stand with him.

Many of those near and dear to them both were on opposite sides in the conflict, and the battles of Shiloh, Atlanta and Vicksburg took their toll of loved ones. When the news came telling of their passing, there was sincere mourning in our home.

Cousin Hala's youngest brother, James, member of a cavalry company, fell from his horse - not from a bullet or shell, but from sunstroke. Although they had been separated for some years, the family tie was strong within her and she deeply mourned his passing, and our family sorrowed with her. The memory of those dark days remains with me, young though I was at the time.

CHAPTER 33

An Open Air Meeting

It was early spring and new wardrobes were necessary for the season. A new dress for each of the two older girls had just been finished, but other things must be provided to make it complete, and one morning mother crossed the river by boat and went up town to make some purchases. On her return she had a bonnet for each of them such as was worn by young girls at that time; a fine straw braid, ribbon and flower trimmed. The front of each bonnet turned back at the face and was filled with flowers. Hala's were dark red roses with buds and leaves, very becoming to her clear olive complexion and dark blue eyes. The crown of each bonnet completely covered the head being tied under the chin with ribbon and the crown trimmed tastefully with bands, loops and bows of the same. Margaret's flowers and ribbons were a rose pink, becoming to her fair complexion and grey eyes. To us those bonnets were stunning. Short silk capes reaching almost to the waistline and a pair of silk lace mitts completed the outfit one might think; but another package was undone and out came two hoopskirts to hold out the skirts of those new dresses. That was "the straw that broke the camel's back" for me. A hoopskirt had been my one great desire. I too had a best dress and while it was not brand new it was still very nice, and all it needed was a hoop-skirt like mother had bought for the girls to show it off to advantage.

My looks at this last display of the purchases mother made must have betrayed my feelings for she immediately said "We cannot buy everything at once" and we knew that was true, as it would take many pounds of the nice butter she made and sold as well as the small earnings of the girls in various occupations, and father must contribute the balance. "Your turn will come next but the older girls must be provided for first."

Sunday morning came and the girls dressed in their new clothes started to church with father. It was Easter Sunday, but I remained at home this time though the family generally all went to church on Sunday mornings and evenings. I watched their departure feeling very forlorn though I shed no tears. Mother was busy finishing the morning work and making preparations for the Sunday dinner, and tidying herself up. Company was expected to come as usual with father and the girls on their return from church and Sunday school.

My brain was working during this time devising ways and means of supplying myself with the needed articles for attending a meeting which I planned to have regardless of any obstacle. First I provided myself with the longed for hoop-skirt by going to the riverbank where so many grapevines were hanging from the trees. Going into the kitchen unnoticed by mother, I secured a strong, sharp butcher knife, and going to the river hunted around until I found a small vine which I proceeded to cut off. After much hard labor this was accomplished. I then trimmed the vine of all its leaves, scraping it clean with the knife, returned to the house, replaced the knife unnoticed by mother who was very busy and went upstairs with my prize. I would have liked to have two grapevines instead of just one but I knew my white skirt was not long enough for a tuck which would be necessary in which to run another grapevine, so I contented myself with the one which I ran in the hem of my skirt.

Next I would need a hat. Then I thought of a straw hat of father's which he no longer wore. It had been his best at one time, a very fine straw, though badly discolored by sweat etc. Securing it I wiped it clean as I could, and with scissors, needle, thread and thimble I climbed into a large box containing cast-off clothing, woolens, worsteds and cotton; all were nice and clean. Selecting from these the color I desired to use as ribbons, I tore strips in the desired width and commenced the trimming; first a band around the crown with loops and bows in the front and back, and two streamers to hang from the bow at the back. Then some of the calico ribbon was sewed on for ties, the hat being too large for my head it wobbled around in a disagreeable manner and the ties would hold it in place. Then I remembered some artificial flowers mother had saved from discarded hats and bonnets, some of which were very nice. I thought a small bunch of flowers could be sewed on in the places where the braid was most discolored and they were scattered around here and there as needed. Sewing through the braid was difficult and the needle sometimes cruelly pricked my fingers. At last it was finished and I held the hat up with a feeling of satisfaction over my skill as a milliner.

I emerged from my cramped position in the rag box and donned the grapevine hoop-skirt, over which I put my best dress. The hoop-skirt I found to be very uncomfortable; the weight of the grapevine caused the underclothing to cling tight to my body while the bottom of the skirt swung around in a disagreeable manner. Placing on my head the hat of my own making, tying the strings under my chin to keep it on, I went quietly down the stairway, taking a testament and hymn book and started to church. On a pile of lumber at the end of some hazel brush close to the fence I thought to hold the services. I must serve as minister, choir and imaginary audience. Climbing on top of the lumber with the testament and hymn book I began the services, offering a prayer and singing a hymn, I began the sermon. Remembering some Bible quotations and using some phrases I had heard some of the minister's use. One in particular had always been very interesting to me; a small man who in his earnestness would wave his arms, pound his fist on the bible stand and hop about on the platform in an athletic manner. I enjoyed his sermons very much, especially the athletic part, though I listened interestingly to all he said, never missing a word, and I tried to copy the Reverend as nearly as possible. There was no bible stand on which to pound my fist and I had to be careful in hopping about on the lumber pile to insure against hopping off.

At last my service was closed by singing a hymn and offering the benediction; I climbed down from the lumber pile and hurried to the house in order to reach there before the arrival of father and the girls with their company, and to remove my toggery, especially the grapevine hoop-skirt which had been so uncomfortable. I dreaded Hala more than anyone; she always saw the funny side of everything and would laugh heartily over it and I did not want to be the victim this time, I was in no humor for it. The non-success of my grapevine hoop-skirt had been a great disappointment and I realized, child though I was, that I must be a ludicrous sight to behold. I hurried to the house and fled in terror up the stairway before being discovered by anyone. Then

I removed the grapevine from my skirt and felt more comfortable. Luck was with me this time and no one knew my secret, the grapevine hoop-skirt and I escaped the humility of being laughed at. Later on mother provided me with the longed for hoop skirt, a new hat with flowers and ribbons and a number of other things making me very happy. I never did forget that Easter Sunday.

CHAPTER 34

Political Meeting

DURING THE SUMMER OF 1863, the many Republicans who were anxious for the nomination of Lincoln for a second term as President had arranged a meeting to be held at Bradford. A speaker had been chosen to deliver the speech which was to be made in the nearly completed Little Brown Church.

The speaker was a returned soldier from the war, a very brilliant and forceful speaker who could hold the attention of his audience with his convincing words. The speaking to be followed by a banquet consisting of a roasted ox, oxtail soup etc. sufficient to serve the large crowd they expected to attend.

Father made preparation to attend this meeting, being very anxious for the nomination of Lincoln for a second term in the Presidency. Taking the two older girls, cousin Hala and sister Margaret and two other girls, friends of theirs along with him. We were satisfied to be left at home with mother. The thought of that poor ox roasted over a fire whole did not appeal to us as at all desirable and oxtail soup "ugh." We were willing to be counted out and no tears were shed by us this time on being left at home although we always counted it a great treat to accompany father anywhere.

A dance at night was to follow these exercises and although no member of our family danced, the night being dark and the roads poor, father left the girls with others who had remained over to return in the daylight. Engaging a room at the hotel for them he departed for home. The room had but one bed and all four girls must occupy it, sleeping crosswise.

Girl-fashion, they tittered and giggled over many things that struck them as very funny, when presently there was a rapping on the wall of the opposite room and a masculine voice said "Less noise in there, please! Some of us would like to sleep." Somewhat chagrined at this reproof, the girls quieted down and soon were in the land of dreams.

Earlier in the evening one of the young boys who had decided to remain over had neglected to engage a room before all were taken. He found the last team had gone and he was faced with the prospect of sitting up alone all night or occupying as a bed a hard bench in the office, minus a pillow or covers. Listening to his tale of woe one of the girls remarked "our room has but one bed, Gobe, and four of us must occupy it, but you might sleep underneath on the carpet." He immediately replied "All right! It's a bargain." Little dreaming that he had meant this, the girls thought no more about it. When the time came to retire and they had lapsed into dreamland the door, not having been locked, was quietly opened and the intruder, who proved to be Gobe, made a lunge and was underneath the bed in an instant. A rattling of china, a splash, and there emerged a red head with dripping locks. The owner, without a word, made a hasty exit through the door and no more was seen or heard from him that night. He was the victim of the joke he had thought to perpetrate on the girls who now wide awake, were stuffing the bedclothes in their mouths to stifle the laughter so hard to suppress. One hint to "make less noise" they did not care to have repeated again that night.

Gobe, it is supposed, was busy giving his head a much needed washing which helped to break the monotony of the long wait for daylight and he was not over-anxious to meet the girls until his hair was dry.

No modern homes those days were known, not even hotels or other public houses; all still used the "chamber pot" for night time, and ours under the bed had caused the humiliation to Gobe. But people were content. They did not miss what they had never had, and we know the saying "Where ignorance is bliss 'tis folly to be wise," though we doubt very much the wisdom of that saying. To be content with things as they were would have meant no progress.

We do not remember what became of Gobe, but hearing no more of him we have thought he might have been one of the boys who had answered a call for volunteers and was among the number who never returned. He had been a general favorite with the young people and all others. Of that jolly foursome of girls none are here today. One by one they have passed on.

CHAPTER 35

Hiring a New Teacher

It was late afternoon in the early fall of 1863. Cousin Hala was busy picking up chips scattered around the rear yard and garden from wood chopping. Having her apron filled, the edges of which she held in her hands, she straightened up from stooping and saw a young man wearing the uniform of the federal soldier who had been watching her at her work. She had not noticed his approach and looked at him in questioning surprise. He politely lifted his hat and asked if Mr. Leonard was home. She answered in the negative and noticing his look of disappointment, she said, "He is downtown but we expect him most anytime as it is near tea time. If you wish to see him you might come inside and wait." Going around to the front door she ushered the young gentleman inside saying to mother, "Aunt Cass, this gentleman wishes to see Uncle Jacob."

Mother greeted him pleasantly and he was seated. She resumed her work trying to cord up a 4 poster bedstead. Noticing what she was trying to do, he arose from his chair and asked if he might assist her, saying: "I think I have more strength in my hands and wrists. That is a difficult job for a woman." Not waiting for an answer he removed his coat, laid it across the back of the chair, pushed up his sleeves, stepped over the bed rail. He reached for the rope which was willingly relinquished as mother began to feel herself unequal to the task. She was feeling impatient over Father not returning in time for his work. Cording bedsteads and doing the heavy lifting at housecleaning time had always been his part of the work. But this time he had tarried too long causing her to feel he had shirked responsibility.

Fastening the rope around the rail by running it through a loop he had made, the young man began to weave it back and forth around the little pegs in rails drawing it tightly. On reaching the head of the bed he fastened his rope firmly again and wove from head to foot forming the little squares so evenly they looked like small windowpanes. In a short time the foundation was ready for the bed tick which had been filled with nice clean straw. Mattresses were unknown at this time.

A covering for this rope foundation was made of heavy white sheeting or canvas and the straw tick was placed on this, then the feather bed without which no bed was considered complete. This was smoothed out evenly and covered with a sheet. Before proceeding further Mother produced a white valance which was draped around to hide the rails and pegs that held the rope. When made up these beds looked as though a ladder would be needed to enable one to climb. They were really very attractive. They always had curtains around them which were looped back through the day showing the beautiful patchwork quilts of woven coverlet whichever might be used. This made it look home-like and comfortable.

Two of these 4 poster beds occupied the south wall of this early Iowa home. The room was very wide, the north side being the living room with a rag carpet, a lounge against the wall with its comfortable cushions, a table on which Mother's basket of sewing or knitting and Father's newspapers on the other end. Some chintz-covered rockers and few other wooden chairs, some shelves on the wall containing books, though the family Bible and Webster's Dictionary were generally found on the table. The clock was on the north wall with a scene of Rome, Italy on the front and at the windows hung white curtains as they furnished better light. Crude as this may seem to some people at the present time it was home and we loved it. We were a happy family and the fact that our home was a log one did not trouble us. Four of the younger sisters were born in this house, Nancy Catherine, Emma Harriett, Lavendee Agnes, and Esther Ellen (the youngest of the family, Clara Aurette was born later in the new house, a frame one).

Well, just as the bed was finished Father arrived home. The young man was introduced and Mother added: "I never would've got the bed together without his help." Father greeted him cordially, thanked him for his kindness to Mother and placing a chair nearby they started a conversation with the usual remarks of the weather, etc. The visitor realizing that much time had already passed stated to Father the purpose of his business. "I understand no teacher has been hired for your school and I wish to put in my application. I have my discharge from the army before my time has expired on account of disability caused by sickness. On leaving the hospital I came west!" Father, I knew, was favorably impressed with the young man's appearance. I could easily see that, child though I was. I could not resist and I anxiously awaited father's answer. "Would it never come" Oh! Why didn't he tell this handsome soldier with the blue uniform and brass buttons he could have our school without waiting so long?"

At last father spoke, saying: "Might I ask if you have credentials? We are strangers to each other and our school has scholars from the primary to those studying the higher academic branches. A mixed school you see, which might be difficult for one not accustomed to such a school."

The young man drew from an inside pocket of his blue soldier coat a folded paper and handed it to father who unfolded it and as he did so a smile overspread his face at a first glance. The paper was the young man's diploma from Harvard University where he had graduated before entering the Army. Father smilingly returned the paper and said: "I see there is no doubt as to your ability to teach the higher studies, but the primaries might be wearisome to one not accustomed to a mixed school." But the young man had no fears of being wearied with the little ones. "I am accustomed to children;" he said, that would be the least of my worries."

Then the length of terms, the salary paid teachers by the District was given by father, all of which seemed satisfactory to the applicant and a teacher was hired for our school, and I was happy at the thought of a soldier teacher.

CHAPTER 36

Playing a School Trick

THE TIME FOR OPENING OF school arrived, and the teacher was pleased to see among his other students the young girl he had met gathering chips for the kitchen fire. He admired her frank and unaffected manner on meeting him so suddenly. He noticed that she was very comely as well. He thought her very unusual and hoped to make her acquaintance at some future date. Finding her here was a pleasing surprise. Time passed and the usual conduct of school and our soldier teacher longed to play court to the girl of the chance meeting. He knew the school room was no place to show preference for any certain one and the teacher must watch his step to avoid criticism. I liked this teacher very much not alone because of the blue uniform, but he seemed to understand children and I felt very kindly toward him. But that did not deter me from wanting to have a little fun at his expense and I argued to myself that he would not punish me because of the fear of offending Hala. I knew he was much interested in her and would do nothing that he thought might displease her. Like a haughty little girl I took advantage for my own amusement.

It was his habit to walk back and forth up and down the aisle. Tall and slender, very straight and military in his bearing, I would watch him in admiration. Amongst my possessions was a small pincushion which I valued. It was a flat little affair about the size of a silver dollar, one side being red and the other blue. The edge was stuck full of pins which were very handy sometimes and I would carry it in my pocket. It had a loop of red ribbons on the edge to hang it up. The thought came to me how funny the cushion would look bobbing about on the edge of the teacher's coattail as he walked about the room. I immediately stuck a pin in the loop for readiness. It was not long until he passed down the aisle near my seat and I reached out and quickly jabbed the pin into his coattail. Unsuspectingly he marched about the room. The younger scholars began tittering and giggling while the older ones were trying to suppress their laughter and the grown-ups could not hide the look of amusement in their eyes. I was very studious during the time seemingly oblivious of what was going on around me. He knew there was something wrong about him and his face took on the blush of a peony. He kept clearing his throat in his embarrassment. In desperation he at last reached his hand behind him trying to discover the cause of all the commotion. He made several unsuccessful attempts in his effort to discover what was wrong. His hand had been reaching too low down to help him in the search for the cause of all the merriment. Reaching higher up it struck the upper edge of the cushion which he immediately removed remembering he had seen me with it he came to my seat and holding it in his palm he said, "I think I shall keep this." He placed it in his pocket and walked away. My heart sank low as I saw it disappear from my sight and I began to wonder if the fun was worth the loss.

CHAPTER 37

Teacher and Cousin Hala

Longing for the chance to play court to the young girl he so much admired, he realized there was little chance for doing so, knowing the school room was no place to show preference for any certain one. The teacher must always watch his step to avoid criticism.

Few avenues there were which afforded young people social interaction. Dances which no one in our family attended were not to be thought of. Church services on Sunday, prayer meeting on Wednesday night (the girls always accompanied my father) gave no young man a chance to offer himself as an escort. No movies in those day, one circus in summer, the 4th of July, a Sunday School picnic once or twice, and the county fair in the fall at which time the girls kept busy looking after one of several booths and serving luncheon in the interest of the church, kept them busy all day. They went home at night all tired out. They had no piano, something very few people did have at that time. But Father purchased a dulcimer for the girls and Hala had become quite proficient and could play a number of pieces very well.

The I.O.G.T. Lodge afforded a chance to mingle socially with the members during intermission. The better element was supposed to belong to this order and they felt at ease mingling freely with all. The teacher had without hesitation allied himself with the lodge, being in full accord with its purpose. This gave him a chance to pay court on the girl of his choosing. His first attempt was to ask to accompany Hala home from lodge one night. She accepted his company and all seemed well. But relating to her aunt next day as was her habit, she said, "When I reached the foot of the stairs the teacher was waiting there and asked to accompany me home and I accepted." Her aunt in whose judgment she had great confidence replied, "He should have asked you before leaving the lodge room and not have waited until you both were out of sight and hearing of others. Next time he or any other young man offers in that way, I would politely refuse them." That was all the advice she needed on the subject. She was in full accord with her aunt's judgment.

On the following Saturday night the teacher was waiting in the same place with no doubt that his company would be accepted. Imagine his surprise and humiliation when Hala said in reply, "I am not in the habit of accepting an escort on the street, thank you," and she sailed on leaving him standing there puzzled at the sudden change.

"There must be a reason for this, and I will ask at the first opportunity." It was not long after this that the time came. The young lady frankly told him of the conversation with her aunt on the manner of his asking to accompany her home and what her aunt had said to her. He quickly understood that he had been in error and apologized saying, "My only excuse is bashfulness. I can make a speech before a crowded house easier that I can ask a girl to see her home. Your aunt was right in saying what she did and it has given me a lesson I needed."

From this time on he became a frequent caller in our home and many pleasant evenings were spent there. Both were good singers and spent much time in that way, singing sacred hymns and war songs, so popular then. In memory I hear their voices as they sang numerous ones, "Tramp, Tramp, Tramp, the Boys are Marching, In a prison cell I sit thinking Mother dear of you," and many others which gave me a thrill. They were both patriotic and sad. Another song they sang sometimes and I loved to hear was "What a joy to press the pillow of a lowly cottage bed and listen to the patter of the soft rain overhead." We would listen as they sang and thought how we enjoyed the patter of the rain as it fell on our shake covered roof. It had been the music that had often lulled me to sleep together the purring of Pussy Cat so often found under the covers with me. It had a soothing effect and soon I would be in dreamland.

All was well for kitty and me until the arrival of the girls on coming to bed. My quiet repose was rudely broken by Hala turning the covers down which she invariably did, exposing kitty. Kitty knowing she was on forbidden ground immediately sprang out of bed and down the stairs, tail erect as she made her flight. Hala had no aversion to cats, was never unkind to them, but she did object having them as a bed fellow. Wide awake by this time, my heart went out in sympathy for kitty, as she loved to crawl under the covers with me. It was so cozy there.

Few games were provided at this time and it was not easy for a girl to entertain her beau for an evening. Card playing in anyone' home was unheard of. They were associated with gamblers only and were not seen outside of a saloon except in Indian wigwams where it was claimed that whoever tried their skill in a game with them left poorer financially and wondering how it had all happened. Now every home has their one or two or more packs of cards without criticism.

Lighting was a problem in my childhood. The tallow candle was our lighting system, and then followed the kerosene lamp, then gas lights, and lastly the electric light (press a button and your lights were on). Surely the world moves a pace. What next I wonder?

CHAPTER 38

A Nations Loss

ON SUNDAY, APRIL 15, 1865, we had company as usual. A family whose house was a couple of miles out of town often came home from church to have dinner and remained for the evening service. During the afternoon the stage came rattling by; the driver was silent, an unusual thing for him, as he always made more or less noise singing and cracking his whip. The stage was heavily draped in black crepe and on the arm of the driver was a band of crepe, and also on the horse's heads. Everyone was deeply concerned at once as to what had happened. Father remarked, "I fear we have lost a battle." Putting on his coat and hat he followed the stage down town to learn what could have been the meaning of the ominous signs. We all waited with anxious dread for his return. At last he was seen coming with bowed head and slow steps. The question on his arrival as to what had occurred was answered when he said, "Our President has been assassinated." Many tears were shed at the appalling news; the day was spoiled and our company went home instead of remaining over as they had intended. The quiet of home was more to be desired now; visiting was out of the question.

Hala had left shortly after dinner to return to her boarding place where she was teaching school in Chickasaw. Each weekend she would come home with someone coming to town and on Sunday afternoon our former soldier-teacher would come with a livery team and take her back. He had now become her regular escort and it was a settled fact in our family that at some future time they would be married. The family liked him as he was a likable young man and he felt very much at home himself with our family.

While still within hearing distance of town they heard a funeral dirge being played with drum and fife. They drove on instead of going to learn what had happened; knowing the news whatever it might be would spread rapidly. On his return, he immediately joined others in arranging a memorial service for the following Sunday, to be held in the court room of the court house in the evening. Speeches were to be made by Patterson and Pratt and several clergymen. All churches were closed and people of all denominations attended the mourning assembly. Feeling was intensely deep. A week later preparation was made for funeral services

Governor Stone had issued a proclamation requesting observance on Thursday April 19, 1865 as a day of prayer in testimony of the sorrow over the assassination of our President. In response, arrangements were made by the citizens of Charles City and vicinity for observance of the day with appropriate ceremonies. They requested that all business be suspended, and the dwelling houses, offices, stores, etc., be draped in appropriate mourning. The citizens of the county assembled in the public square at Charles City at 10:00 am, formed procession and marched to the court house where religious services were held, conducted by the several clergymen of the county. An oration was delivered by H.O. Pratt on the death of our President, Abraham Lincoln, being delivered in his usual earnest and patriotic manner.

Dark days followed. People were greatly depressed over the nation's loss and business was almost at a standstill for a time. They felt uncertain of the future since the loss of their leader and seemed unmanned by this stunning blow. But to continue for long in this state of mind is not characteristic of American citizenry. They continued to carry on for the good of the country, even though confronted by many difficulties and discouragements caused by the perfidy of someone unworthy of the name, American Citizen. A Christian nation, she had survived by the guidance of The All Wise One and she still carried her nation's banner aloft.

CHAPTER 39

We Grow Old

My friend Mary became acquainted with and was afterward married to a young man from the East and commenced housekeeping on a farm not far distant from her sister Anna where most of her childhood had been spent after the death of their mother.

Her farm home was on land her father had reserved for her during his lifetime having given each of his children sufficient land for a good-sized farm. She remained there until after the death of her sister, Ann, when they sold their farm home and removed to a neighboring town. She said to me one day, "I just could not stand to live there after Ann was gone. I was too lonely. Otherwise we never would have left that home as it was very dear to us."

This was our first separation since meeting in early childhood, and we were now elderly women. A lifetime spent together, one might say, with no shadow between during the years. No closer tie of friendship could there be than was ours which reminds me of some lines I read early in life:

> *There are two souls who equal flow,*
> *In gentle streams they calmly run,*
> *And when they part, they part—ah no!*
> *They cannot part, those souls are one.*

I have almost forgotten to say that I too had married, for "Dan Cupid" is an old traitor to all would-be old maids, which we both had resolved to be. But he captured me in an unguarded moment and I soon found myself in that sometimes turbulent sea of matrimony. Of course it was not my fault! I merely said "yes" as quickly as the poor fellow asked, and he had no time to change his mind if he had wanted to. Father said, on having been informed of this happening, "Now, young man, you shall work seven years for this girl as

Jacob did for Rachel. I am not ready to relinquish my claim on her for some years to come."

Many years have passed since these happenings and gone with the years are most of our beloved ones and many familiar faces we no longer see. Among them the young man I said "yes" to in the early seventies.

The farm homes of us all are now within the town site and little is left of the familiar scenes where many happy hours were spent with those of my childhood. Pleasant memories still are with me after so many years.

MARY'S PERSONAL CORRESPONDENCE

*L*ETTER WRITTEN BY *MARY E. Leaman, to welcome her granddaughter, Mary Jane Leaman to the world:*

Broken Arrow, Oklahoma
Jan. 25, 1915

My Dear Little Mary Jane:

Think that grandma will write you the first letter; the older ones can wait until I write my own girl and tell her how glad grandma was to hear that she had arrived to make glad the hearts of Papa and Momma and all the rest of us. We shed tears when we got your card, but they were tears of joy, and a prayer went up to Heaven that our little girl might always remain the pure and sweet flower which God gave into the care of father and mother and when He calls her Home may she be ready to answer God's call and gladly return. But God will have work for little Mary Jane and may she be His willing servant, and the world is better for her having lived is the prayer of her grandmother.

To both of you, Charlie and Lucile:

Cherish this precious gift of your Heavenly Father, and guide the little footsteps in the right, keeping in mind the obligation to Him who has entrusted her to your care. May He guide and help you to do your duty by little Mary Jane and make her a Christian woman.

Best love to you all,
Mother

Letter written by Mary E. Leaman to son, Charlie and family:

Charles City, Iowa
March 1st, 1929

Dear Charlie and Family:

Forty-one years ago today another boy was added to the Leaman Flock. Grandma Allen said, "I have taken care of 150 babies and this is the worst one of all. You will just have to get another nurse; one cannot do it all, night and day." The echo of those cries did not entirely cease for three months and after that I had the best baby ever. And I still wonder what could have ailed him. But you have been lots of comfort to mother, and we don't regret the extra work and worry you made them. May you live to a good old age and a comfort to Lucile and the girls.

God bless my boy.
Lovingly, Mother

Letter written by Mary E. Leaman.

Charles City, Iowa
May 2nd, 1929

My Dear Children:

Excuse the use of lead pencil, but feel that I cannot wait longer for the day to come when I might not be so nervous. I want to thank you for your very generous birthday gift. It makes me very happy when my children remember mother's birthday. And I'm hoping you're not robbing yourselves by so generous a remembrance. I can use it all right, and made a payment on some new teeth I had to get. It will not be many years, I hope, until I can have the income from the little cottage to use as I please. Have kept on with improvements and have used none of the money except for improvements and paying out on it, interest, etc. I have never lost a week's rent yet. So far, there is always someone ready to take the other fellows place. Only two parties have occupied it so far. The first family to occupy it bought a home last fall, and I was swamped with applicants, and not a day's rent was lost by the change in tenants. Pretty lucky, wasn't I? Have put in a furnace and now have hot and cold water and this spring I had new cement walks put in and things are looking real nice, even tho' the house is a little old-fashioned one. Only wish I could be the tenant myself and have my children coming home to "Mother's."

We are well now, but we each had our turn at not being so this winter.

I want to thank Lucile and the girls for their nice letters and the snapshots of you all. The funny part was someone had pasted a chicken on the back of Charlie's picture, so we saw the chicken instead of seeing him, and tho' perhaps he was not in the party when the pictures were taken and just had the chicken on for a joke. Sometime after, I got the letter and the pictures out to look at again and lo, there was my "Toddy Boy" looking as tho' he had not a care in the world. All that time, and I had not discovered him. They all laughed and took a turn looking at the picture which they all had missed. The pictures all were good, but my girlies have grown so, I can hardly realize it is them. All look as tho' they were well fed, and guess Charlie's cookin' is not impairing their health any. Wish we might fly over the miles and light in there someday. I get lonesome many times to see my children, all. Maybe someday, our "ship will come in" and then our fondest hopes will be realized.

Had a nice letter from Laura for my birthday and she enclosed a postal order for ten dollars, and we began to think it was raining money from my children out in Washington.

Went downtown a few days ago and Daisy Morris came running out from her house to greet me, and I was real glad to see her, as it had been some time since I had seen her. As usual, she is looking well and happy, and of course, she asked about you all.

Mary and her baby are still at Vera's. She intended staying only two weeks, but the baby has the "whooping cough" and all thought she had better stay at home a little longer. Suppose Aaron will be anxiously waiting for them. She has a very pretty baby.

Bye-bye, lots of love to all my dear ones.
Mother

Letter written by Mary E. Leaman to son, Charlie and family:

Charles City, Iowa
Dec. 18th, 1930

My Dear Children:

A long mail, this, in answering your nice letter, received so long ago. They are most welcome to me even tho' I am so slow in answering them. You can see by my writing it's not an easy matter to write a letter to any of you; but your mother does not forget her children, and in memory I see each one as in the days long gone by when you all were at home. "Dreaming," you will call it, perhaps, but nevertheless I see you all as you were then.

One little happening, a few days before Christmas, I had my meager shopping done, and was feeling pretty good in that I had each one of you provided for; dolls for the girls (Myrta and Madge); a horn for Roy; a little white lamb for Vera, the baby, then about two years old, and which she always carried around with her, and calling it "my sheepie lamb." Well, these things were carefully stored away in a trunk in one of the bedrooms, waiting for Christmas Eve. All, of course, knew Mama had been to town to see Santa Claus, and were curious to know what was in store for each one, and Myrta, being the eldest, and a little more adventuresome than the rest, opened the trunk, just for a peep at the things she knew must be in there, when Roy, having discovered the horn, a bright red cord around it, with tassels hanging, like lightening he grabbed it, and before the girls could take it from him had blown a blast on it that told mother what was going on and here we came comb in hand, and regardless of breaking it (we were combing our hair at the time) used it for a paddle, to impress each one to desist from meddling. Myrta never forgot it. She said to me one day, not long before she passed away; "Mamma, do you remember the time we children opened the trunk to see our Christmas things, and Roy grabbed the horn and blew that terrible blast, Oh, Mamma, I never had such a shock in my life, it seemed no horn could ever give such a blast as that one did." It could not have been later than the year 1881. We were living in Mrs. Craig's cottage, had not yet built our house, and I doubt if Roy can remember, tho' he may,' but it always remained in the memory of the girls, who never forgot.

Love, Mother

A letter from Mary E. Leaman to her son, Charles and Lucile Leaman, who were living in Longview, Washington, and owned a restaurant, "Leaman's Lunch" at this time. Mary refers to this business in her letter. Letter also addressed to "grandchildren" (Betty and Jane).

Charles City, Iowa
Dec. 22, 1931

My Dear Children and Grandchildren,

We will try to write this letter but am using a lead pencil and hope it will be acceptable. Have not heard from any of you in a long time, I know I do not write very often myself, but it is hard for me to do so, and someday perhaps you'll understand. We are not censuring you, for we know how busy you both are; and am glad you went into the business you did, for people must eat, if money is scarce, and it will enable you to make a living anyhow.

We look at the paper with the business men's pictures, which you send every once in a while, and of course gaze long at our "Toddy Boy" and wonder why Lucile's picture was not in there, too. Guess we women don't count for much, even tho' we are allowed to cast our vote. We're just as important, in our own opinion, are we not? And, like one of my neighbors, years ago said to me when she thought some of the folks were displeased at her for something she had said or done; "If they don't love me, I'll love myself." And that's what we'll have to do, won't we?

How are my two little girls coming? Alright, I hope. Looking over some of the old letters and saw where Jane had given some of her grades or studies, and they certainly were good.

Jan. 6, 1932

This letter, began the 22nd of Dec., 1931, we are not going to throw away (too hard to write) as we were interrupted in the midst of it and was unable to go on with it, so much interference, first one thing then another. Last, but not least, I had to think "I'm sick." I was almost cheated out of my Christmas and New Year's dinner. But I was up and at the table with the rest of them; ate dressing, but had to touch light on the meat. Turkey for Christmas and lovely chickens for New Year's, hard telling which dinner was best both were certainly good. Ruth and Mel were with us both times; and had Elaine with them over New Year's.

I must not forget to tell you that we enjoyed opening the packages from you people, Mother, of course was "officer of the day," in handing each one their share of the chili you sent, etc. Madge cooked ours one night for a late feast. Ruth, Mel and Vera were here; had been playing cards, and Madge thought to give them a late lunch, so cooked our chili. I went to bed, but had some the next day, and it was certainly good and I enjoyed it. Kit and Roy Sours were going to let Art Briscoe's in on theirs, and have it together, as they seem always to do.

The holly you sent was certainly beautiful; and the pictures made mother's heart glad. They were good, very good. Just one thing missing, where was Lucile to make it complete? Just take time off and get yours taken, little lady, and send it along to make the Leaman family group complete.

Grandmother made some mats for hot dish pads to save your dining tables, some day in the future, they will be useful as well as a reminder that one day, you had a grandmother who loved you well enough to do this work for you – my two little girls out west. Ruth took them with her to New Hampton Monday morning when she went to her work and was going to mail them out from there for me. Ruth is always ready to do anything for grandmother. You can call them birthday presents, graduation or anything you wish. I made them both to make sure you would have them. But don't think you must hurry up and get married, for they'll keep. Just put them in your cedar chests, they were not addressed to each of you and you can each take a set. They are just alike near as I could make them.

Good bye, with love,
Mother and Grandmother

Letter written my Mary E. Leaman to her son, Charles Leaman and his wife, Lucile and her two granddaughters, Betty and Jane.

Charles City, Iowa
March 15, 1935

My Dear Children and Grandchildren:

I'm wondering if I will be able to write this letter without making a "nose dive." Am capitalizing a verb as tho' it was a proper noun, and if that is the only mistake I make it will be a wonder. Have spoiled one sheet of paper by making the dive, so have begun drawing lines to avoid another. Like the lined sheets best, as for some reason, I cannot avoid the "dive."

Am thinking you have wondered why we had not written long before this, in acknowledgment of that wonderful Christmas present you sent to me. I opened the envelope and when I saw what it contained I was, as the Irishman would say, "speechless." Certainly was not looking for such a liberal handout as that was. And I wonder if mother was really worthy of such a generous gift. Felt like having it framed and hung on the wall. Mothers are sometimes paid for having had children, and in my last days, as the sun is going down on 81 years of a life—which I wish I might say had been more worthwhile, as I can think of nothing very great having been accomplished, but am hoping that something, even at this late hour, may yet be accomplished that might be of benefit to someone. Am hoping the next generation accomplishes more in a general way than I have. My children and grandchildren mean so much to me in these last years. Life would seem void, indeed, if I was left alone in the world with no one of my own. Ponder this, girls and be ready to "multiply and replenish the earth." That means if you marry, and I have no doubt but that you will when the time comes. Looks as tho' you both would be "good pickins." And your daddy may have to sit in the doorway with a shot gun across his knees if he counts on keeping you many years. That is the value grandmother places on her granddaughters. Is the rating too high? Say "no."

'Tis snowing today, and looks now as tho' there might be more good sleighing. It will do no harm after too much draught as we had last summer; the moisture is certainly welcomed by all, or should be.

The river raised quite a bit a week or so ago, tho' the ice above the dam is still intact, so they say; melting slowly from underneath without breaking up as it usually does, and then some people are foolish enough to imagine it sinks. Have heard them say that very thing. Just let them try to sink a piece of ice, and they will be the first one to accomplish such a feat. Old Rover, Beardsmore's dog, was standing on the walk, looking down toward the river, and nearly barking his head off. It was rising fast, and caused some uneasiness with us; and think he remembered the experience of two years ago, when they and a number of other families had to leave their homes, and he was acting in the role of Paul Revere, and rousing the countryside to impending danger. Don't think for a minute that dogs are not wise.

Commenced this letter several days ago, but cannot afford to cast it aside (too hard to write). Well, the river is clear of ice now, and the water is receding, and I think we'll not catch fish at the 4-corners this year.

Lucile, I tried to make you a handkerchief which I am sending in this letter. 'Tis not new, the cloth, but was nice in its time, so just use it and if it doesn't last very long, perhaps I can make you another one someday—am going to send Laura one from the same piece of cloth. Am almost afraid to offer it to her; but 'tis the best I can do now with my stiff fingers.

Betty's pictures which you sent me in her different dresses do not look much like the one I enclosed with Charlie's birthday greeting. Will it give her a swelled head if grandmother says she is a "fine looking young lady?" And Charlie's pictures with the fruits of his hunting trip, and standing with his gun, made us think him a good replica of Daniel Boone. Ronald wanted to show those pictures to

John Webster, who he says asks so often about Charlie, but he has not done so yet. And to think of anyone ever living in that lonely cabin out in the wilds, and why didn't they leave some record of their lives there? If only the old cabin could talk it might make interesting history. Wonder if it was a family or a man alone. Suppose we'll continue to wonder and never know. What could cause anyone to go so far from human habitation, and yet, much of this country never would have been settled had someone had not had the urge to explore.

Went to the movies with Madge last night. The first time I have gone in several years. Ronald took us up in a car, or I couldn't have gone. Enjoyed it very much—not a tragedy, or I wouldn't have gone. Shirley Temple, in The Little Colonel, and I always have liked the Southern scenes. And she certainly is a real little actress.

Faye will never forget her Washington visit with all of you when she was out there and hopes to go again before she comes back here, to again "lite on a pancake." That is how it seemed to me when I came back after six months of Washington's beautiful scenery. Well, I had six months of great pleasure seeing the beautiful scenery, and should be content, but we would have liked a squint of the old ocean and hear it roar.

Must close, I'm getting tired and fear you will be tired too. When I get wound up I never know when to stop.

Much love to all my dear ones.
Mother

Another letter written by Mary E. Leaman to her children: In it she describes early life in the log house they used to live in when they first came to Charles City.

Charles City, Iowa
Dec. 30, 1935

Mary's Story

Dear Children and Grandchildren:

Should send this by airplane but we are just too stingy, not knowing just what might happen to our generous income—one never knows. It certainly has been like manna from the skies, and how we do thank you. What would mother do now, without her children and grandchildren? Many, many thanks for all those surprise packages, on top of the cash. Mother should be happy as some little child whose faith in "Old Saint Nick" has not yet been shattered, and we do strongly believe in all parents affording their children the great pleasure of the mystery of "Old Saint Nick." The surprises this year carried us back to early childhood when we were awakened late at night, and by the candlelight in the room could see an arm reaching up, filling our stockings, pinned to the curtains enclosing our bed, as was the custom in those days, not so much thought given about "fresh air" as now days, and yet we lived, and still are living at the age of nearly 82 years, minus the "fresh air" which we think so necessary to our existence; and I believe I prefer to breath it now, but ignorance is bliss 'tis folly to be wise, but we are glad to breath fresh air these days.

    The log building which was our early home, had been a store, consequently no windows on the sides, and two beds had been placed end to end on one side wall, while the other beds were upstairs. Those downstairs being curtained off left the balance of the space for a living room, whichever you choose to call it; a rag carpet on the floor, a table on which was a candlestick with the snuffers, father's newspapers, the family Bible, a dictionary, mother's sewing basket, knitting, etc. (for she was never idle), some chairs, rockers, etc. The walls, mother had papered with newspapers, in lieu of wallpaper, a map of the U.S.A., a shelf on which stood the clock, a bunch of beautiful peacock feathers which mother had brought with her from Wisconsin. In the winter time a heating stove stood near the center of the floor, as in all store buildings, distributing the heat more evenly to all parts of the room. A very wide door in front, with a wooden latch, to which was a leather string, drawn inside at night for safety. That was the means they had of locking up the store at night, on retiring to the room at the rear of the building, and this was our kitchen and dining room. Two windows on each side of the wide front door, store style, afforded all the light for that part of the house, a platform in front of the door, the "stage road," as we called it. Hazel brush in front, across the road, from which we gathered our supply of hazelnuts for winter. A large log building, about one block distant, and a little more to the south, had been built by an Ohio family—always spoken of (the man) as "Esquire Hackley." He was a white-haired, elderly man; his wife, much younger, having two boys by a former marriage, the eldest boy, about Will's age, and a nice companion for him, in his otherwise isolated life. A narrow path leading through the hazel brush between the two houses was the only road and it was well traveled. One other log house, or I might say two, facing each other, and an alley between the two, doors facing each other, one roof covering all; very small windows, high up at the sides, supposedly to prevent Indians from looking inside at the occupants as was their habit, when the windows were in reach; pressing their faces against the pane so closely as to flatten their noses in doing so. They were always in their native garb; leather leggings, and moccasins, blanket and always the feathers in the band around their head.

 This double log house was in the timber back of our house, with a narrow cut thru' the timber leading to it; joining the only street then laid out and running over what we since have spoken of as "Court House Hill," now South Main. So Court House then, no church. A few graves in the timber on the hillside, to the right of the roads, where a few early burials had been made, before a cemetery was laid out and one little girl, the first death to occur was buried in the timber, where the court house was afterward built and I suppose her little bones are still there; her people having left the country before a cemetery was laid out; and now, of course, no one knows the exact spot and she is just as safe. They went farther west and it was reported that her father had been killed by the Indians as had been so many others.

We had plenty of wild berries in those early days: raspberries and strawberries galore. And Oh! The nice shortcakes mother used to make. No fruit cans in those days, so we feasted while berries lasted, and waited for the next year.

Love to all my dear ones,
Mother

Letter written by Mary E. Leaman to her son, Charles Leaman and Lucile: It must have been written shortly after she returned from a visit to see Charlie and Lucile in their new home in Washington State.

Charles City, Iowa
April 6, 1936

My Dear Children and All,

Back again to the old address, after more than a year of one of the greatest pleasures of our life, seeing the wonderful sights of the great state of Washington; pictures of which we shall carry in memory the rest of our life. Scenery so varied and wonderful and we thank you for giving us this greatest pleasure of our life. And we realize more than ever how beautiful are God's creations.

We long to lie on the sands by the ocean deep,
and hear the wild waves
lull the mermaids to sleep
in their caverns deep.
by Mary Eliza Leaman

We arrived in Mason City Friday morning, where we found two or three autos waiting for us. Martin and Madeline had remained over an extra day to greet us before going on Omaha, and Kit and Roy Sours were there with their new Dodge car and I rode home in their car. All celebrated our home coming together at Cad's that first day, and we had an enjoyable time with them all, despite being tired from our long trip.

The railroads were faithful in their efforts to make us comfortable. Many of the passengers were vigilant in their attentions to us, and we parted with some of them with regret after our short acquaintance.

Shortly after boarding the train at Portland, we had a little jolt when a lady whose berth was next to ours greeted us with the announcement that the train had been robbed a few nights before, and advised us if we had any extra money or valuables we had better take precaution for their safety. We thanked her for the information, and when we retired put all bills, except a few small ones, inside our night clothes, taking the purse with the small amount left in it inside the bed with us as tho' to safeguard the little bit left in it. We did not lie awake watching for robbers, but went to sleep thinking the stunt would not be repeated on the same train, for a time at least.

We had noticed on entering our car, signs posted warning passengers that the railroad company would not be responsible for any losses incurred. And we have wondered if it was for that reason, tho' we know some people are careless at all times, locking the barn door after the horses are stolen.

Tho' the C.M. and St. Paul Railroad would have brought us with our baggage to Charles City with but one change we are not sorry, because the scenery was all different over this road, and very beautiful. This does not mean that the other scenery was not beautiful over the other road, but gave us a chance to see both.

We went up to Margaret's the next day and saw them all, and all seemed glad at the prodigal's return.

Pass this around with our love to all. It is miserably written but we just can't help it.

Our love to the café force; we will never forget them and their many kindnesses to us, and goodies they used to cook—rhubarb, barley and vegetable soups. And the onions Mrs. Germo used to fix for us the way we like them.

Recv'd the coffee, and it smelled good but the coffee cooker we had bought at Aberdeen was broken in transit, and of course, we will try to keep the coffee from losing its strength until we can use it. Thanks.

We recv'd hats, etc. which you sent so prompt, all in good shape, and that light weight summer hat certainly looked good to us in this terrible heat they are having at this time.

Grandmother will miss her Janey and Betty, both so dear to us, and my Lucile and Charlie.

Madge is very poorly. Think Cad plans on taking her to the hospital at Rochester this fall.

Will say good-bye with much love to all; Cad is waiting to mail the letter for us.

Love again, Mother

Letter written by Mary E. Leaman to her granddaughter, Mary Jane Leaman.

Charles City, Iowa
March 16, 1938

My Dear Granddaughter and hers:

Please do not think that we did not appreciate your nice letter written us so long ago, because we had not answered sooner. We have almost worn it out with reading and rereading it so many times. Every word is precious to grandmother, and we still keep it. When Clare Sours Leek was here to bid us good-bye as they were leaving to make their home in Montana, she was much pleased to read it and copied your address and I suppose you have heard from her 'ere this.

Much has happened since we left dear old Washington where we spent so many happy months.

Your Aunt Marge is still confined to her bed, tho' she is coming all right slowly. Cad has been an excellent nurse, and very faithful. He stays right by his post.

And what would they do without your aunt Faye? She carried on the household, and prepares the food for the sick as well as for the rest of us. If you ask what grandmother does toward making herself useful, we will say "it is keeping from under foot of those who are doing something." Our movements are too slow for the younger generation, and we help them most by keeping out of the way. Now they do not say that, and we are not complaining, but we are not so dumb that we do not realize we are no longer necessary as a helper. We have had our day, and now must step aside and let the younger ones.

Thankful we are that our room is comfortable and light. And we can see to read, write, darn our socks and crochet.

We still are writing on our history of the long ago. The more we write, the more comes to our mind, and if we could run a typewriter would get through much sooner, and not have to burden others with the typing.

You must know that Ruth and Marian Stoeber are both in Oakland, California and Ruth is going to remain as she now has a position which pays her more money. Marian also has a job and Ruth now intends to send for Elaine to finish her school courses there. Lucky she was to have Elaine with so nice a family as the Olson's while she has been away.

Too bad that Ruth's last matrimonial venture went on the rocks as it did. But I was not surprised after witnessing what I did when I was visiting them. So much that was commendable about him aside from drink, it is truly pitiful, and each time afterward he would be so penitent and beg everyone's forgiveness, and the last of each week it would be repeated, and it was really dangerous for anyone there. Their life was in danger. He was maniacal when under the influence of the curse to all mankind. I was greatly disappointed in him, as I really liked him when he was himself.

Seems as tho' this letter is a doleful one, and think we had better stop before we cause you to have bad dreams by its perusal. Did your father receive his birthday letter? We had no nice card to send, and wrote a letter instead. He never writes me—your mother has been the "good Samaritan." She writes once in a while and we always enjoy her letters.

How is Betty? Our love to her.

Love and best wishes to both.
Grandmother

Letter written by Mary E. Leaman to her son Charles D. Leaman and wife, Lucile:

Charles City, Iowa
April 21, 1938

My Dear Children and Grandchildren:

We were very happy to receive your letters on our natal day, and read them, devouring every word as a hungry wolf might devour some meat. Your letters mean much to mother; 'tis the next thing to seeing you.

The snow and ice are now gone and everything looks nice and green. Fruit trees all in bud, and it looks promising if Jack Frost keeps his nose out of things, but he is a sly old coot, and one never knows when he may creep in and spoil it all. Well, we shouldn't worry it gets one nowhere, but here is hoping he will not.

We received the holly you sent, and the chili which we all enjoy so much, and the elk horn which you had finished up so nicely. We are thanking you now if not before; I was under the impression that I had acknowledged receiving them long ago. Perhaps I dreamed it.

You folks must not eat too many fish, or you will be growing fins.

Remember me to Everett and wife, and hope they enjoy their visit as much as I did mine. They should get an eye-full and carry the memory home with them.

Hope Janey and Eddie have good luck following advice from their cookbooks; and Betty, I expect will be sewing up everything with that new sewing machine. She can sew the rips up in Daddy's pants, and make Mother a new dress.

Remember me to the Café force. I will be writing them a "thank you" for the nice cards I received on our Easter birthday.

Our love to everyone, cats, parrots and even the dog that followed me home and right through the door as I opened it. And stood at the top of the stairs looking down at me as tho' tickled over the joke he played on me, by tagging me home. He knew I did not want him, the scamp!

Sorry to hear of the accident which robbed Eddie's sister of her husband. The automobiles take their toll of lives equal to war, and yet we would hate to do without them.

Love to all. Mother

Mary's Story

Another letter written by Mary E. Leaman to her son, Charles D. Leaman and Lucile:

Charles City, Iowa
Dec. 28, 1938

My Dear Children:

Santa Claus was very nice to us, sending so many goodies to us. We thought when the first package arrived containing the chili etc. we ceased to expect him a second time, when Lo! here they came a second time with all that nice fruit, first a box of nice apples, then a basket of grapefruit followed by another basket half-full of more nice looking oranges, etc. and finished their delivery with a box of mother's favorite loaf sugar and a sack of horehound candy. It would have needed to be a whale of a stocking to hold all that Santa left. We failed to hear the jingle of his bells, but we got the goods all right. We'll not draw the latch string in on Xmas night, tho' he may pass us up next year and do for someone else. However, all had a good laugh over Santa's donation. Thank you!

The past few days we have been having some genuine winter weather, and we had a real white Christmas with all the trimmings. Prior to that, the weather had been very mild for this season of the year. Old Jack Frost has certainly been showing his teeth and he will have two months or more in which to give us a plenty. Hope we may have an early spring with no return visit to freeze the budding trees etc.

Kitty Johnson has closed her nice home after selling most everything in it and has gone to spend some of the time in Des Moines with Marian and family. Before Will Johnson died he mortgaged the property—both places heavily, in order to provide an annuity for Kit, relieving her of the worry and expense of looking after things. Each month, during her life, she will receive a certain sum for her needs. Will Johnson's health failed and he was almost blind with no hope of recovering his sight, and perhaps passing was a blessed release to him.

He was one man in a thousand who spend his life doing for others. He was a good son-in-law to Margaret and it is well she passed on before this trouble came upon them.

Jake Gange's eyesight is about gone, and he gets a pension for the blind. And you can see things are not as rosy as they once were. Jake's wife left hope shortly after Margaret's passing. She knew Jake could do no more for them, and she needed a set of teeth; hers had been removed long before, and she also was in need of glasses to protect her eyesight. She took a job of nursing the sick in Waterloo, where Rob is employed, and the last I heard she was doing housework.

I spent about 3 weeks in Minneapolis visiting Essie. She appears to be failing physically, not the Esther she once was. Much of her trouble is discouragement, I think. She always did so much for others it seems she is deserving of better than the fates have handed her. Rollin is with her at present; for how long I do not know. He has just finished writing a book on the early settlement of Minnesota, Indian troubles, etc. Some of which I could remember hearing of when very young. Rollin has had to read extensively and study hard to be able to get it ready for the publishers. He insisted on my reading it as he typed it and was very pleased when I told him that many of his narratives were correct as I had remembered them, and he said "Aunt Mary, when I have finished my work I will be glad to type yours ready for the publishers." His is Minnesota history while mine is Iowa. A friend of his, financially able, will have the book published for him and that will save infringement on the copyright. In that he is spared where mine must be protected beforehand. I do so hope he can type it for me as I write it. No danger of infringement on anything except the historical part which Rollin says is valuable. How I wish I could type, tho' if Rollin can do it for me it is safe.

Madge is coming along fine and how thankful we are after many months of anxiety and being informed by the Doctors' her case was hopeless, and the end would be soon. But do not think we did not study

Science and Health up in our room during all this time. Sly about it too, much opposition. We kept our books out of sight, all except the Bible, which would not be questioned. Madeline was the only one who knew, and God be praised, she lived, despite all, and is doing fine.

Did you receive the Charles City paper Faye sent containing as article I wrote of Decoration Day in 1874? Kit Johnson went to the office for some extra copies for the folks in Chicago, and was told they were all gone. Cad bought the last ones they had and they were sent to Charlie and Roy because they had known Craig's boys. Roy Sours said he was in the office and they were greatly pleased with the article, and asked him if he thought they might get me to contribute something for the paper once in a while. Said he told them I was busy writing some early day history.

When you write, tell me how Everett and wife liked the Great Northwest. We do not wonder that so any two-legged bears now inhabit that far-away country. And we are in love with it our self—always will be.

Our love to Grace and hers, to Sunny faced Ernest and Hattie, Mark and the boys, in fact the whole Hollis outfit. I often think of them in the long ago when the family was all in their Tulsa home, and Lucile running around with her paper dolls and jack straws.

Bye-bye, Love to all. Mother

Letter written my Mary E. Leaman to her son, Roy Leaman, in 1939: Roy Leaman was Charles D. Leaman's brother. Interesting comments in here about Mary not liking her middle name "Eliza:"

Charles City, Iowa
August 19, 1939

Dear Children:

Winifred Castillo, Ronald's wife, came with her car and took me uptown to sign these papers. Sorry there has been such a mix-up over your real name given you by me when you were a young babe, which was Leroy Stanly, and should have been so recorded in the bible. Of course, we always called you Roy, for short, omitting the "Le," and as you became older you, for some reason, seemed to have an aversion to the name while I had always liked it, especially Stanly, which you seemed to detest, and you have gone thru' life it seems as Roy S. Leaman. Perhaps your marriage license and certificate both bear that name, and if so, it must continue on as Roy S. Leaman. I see no other way.

I never liked my name Mary Eliza, especially the Eliza part of it. Thought I was named for two aunts, neither of whom I needed to feel ashamed, I just did not like the name somehow.

Charlie and Lucile sent me some Longview papers containing much interesting history of that country's settlement. I have enjoyed reading them.

Have not been doing very much on the past history of happenings in Charles City, tho' I hope to finish it someday whether it amounts to anything the future outcome will disclose. I have been handicapped on account of not being able to do my typing myself, but here is hoping.

Faye sent you a paper containing some of my writing published in the Press which seemed to interest some of its readers, who asked me to contribute more, but I can't very well do much of that, though I may give them some more.

'Tis raining today, a steady downpour, and the earth seems to drink it all up, and soon the dust will be flying again.

What do you think? Winifred caught a large Pickerel one day last week at their home in the old Fairgrounds, a regular old-timer, such as we caught here in the very early days. It must have escaped the anglers for many years, to be caught at last by a woman. She was assisted by her mother in bringing it safely to the shore. They claim its weight was 25 lbs. However, it alone served quite a number of people, who enjoyed this rare fish of the present. This news belongs in Ripley's column "Believe It or Not!" This may be disputed by some people at the present time, though I remember when those very large Pickerel were caught here in the Cedar, and "seeing is believing." I cannot imagine how that one escaped the anglers for so many years. It should have been brought into town, weighed and put on exhibition where people could see it themselves, then there would be no doubt as to its size and weight.

I had hoped to finish this letter and get it in the mail this morning, but company came and it was laid aside.

Love to you both and best wishes. Mother

Letter written by Mary E. Leaman to her son, Charles D. Leaman and Lucile:

Charles City, Iowa
Jan. 23, 1940

Dear Children:

I am wondering if I had written you since receiving that Christmas shower of nice fruit, etc. Seems to me I had, but have been so uncertain it has worried me. How about it? Had I or had I not done so? However it is I've enjoyed it greatly.

The passing of your uncle Will Gange on New Year's day and the children all coming here, all of them, at Madge's here together until after his burial, has left me at sea on everything, I wonder if I'll ever be righted.

His children all caressed me, both boys and girls, and said "Oh, Aunt Mary, you are all we have now, and we do love you." The children were all there except Grace and Rob, and there was a bunch of them. Our families are becoming fewer and fewer as time passes. There are more of your Aunt Margaret's family left, having been no deaths since they lost their first boy in 1872.

I try to work at times on my history, hoping to finish it someday and feel as tho' I'd turn a somersault even if I am nearly 86 years old. The typing of it has been very slow for various reasons. The one typing it says I already have enough for a good size book. Am now writing the account of Morgan's and Jennison's raids during the Civil War, and that comes close at home to us. One of the victims of Morgan's raid was an uncle of your grandmother Leonard. She visited them during the seventies a few years after the war. Aunt Evelyn Berkey told her all about their harrowing experiences during the raid. After reading Margaret Mitchell's book "Gone with the Wind" in which she portrays Morgan as a hero and martyr, knowing what I do, I feel the real unbiased facts should be given to the public. What she says is misleading and gives one a wrong impression. It makes more work but I feel it is my duty, knowing the real facts. Jennison was just as bad as Morgan even tho' he was on the Union side.

'Tis bedtime so will say Good Night. Love to all. Mother

Letter written by Mary E. Leaman to her son, Charlie Leaman and his wife, Lucile:

Charles City, Iowa
Mon., July 28th, 1941

My Dear Children, Charlie and Lucile:

I am enclosing an article published in the Charles City Press, July 3rd. It is late in coming to you but hope it will be welcome. There are some errors in it which I have tried to correct. One place in which the Press said the celebration was in the southwest part of town, it was in the south part, between the courthouse and the Freeman log building, our early home. This was the first building in what is now Charles City, built in 1852, by Robert Freeman, and in it was the first P.O. in what is now Floyd County, mail being brought twice each week by stage. Too bad this building was torn down, it should have been preserved. People did not seem to realize the importance of such things. No one here at the time it was built except Indians, though Mr. Kelly had come here in 1850, he resided in a tent until 1854, when he build a log cabin on the north side of the river, moving his family here in the spring.

The roof of our early home was covered with shakes in lieu of shingles, since no saw mill was here. Our family came in June 1857, though father came out in 1856, bought 160 acres of land from the Government, returned to Wisconsin, taught two terms of school the following winter, stored our goods in the school house at the end of the last term and brought the family to our new home in Iowa. We had to return the next year for our goods. The country here was full of wild animals at this time. Buffalo, elk, deer, bear, cougars, wolves, both prairie and timber wolves, and their howls at night were frightening to me and I would cover my head at night with the bedclothes. Hunters from the East were killing them off--buffalo, bear, elk, deer and many other animals. I know they were still here because a buffalo jumped over my head as I was sitting in the door-yard of our home the first summer here. I was sitting still, not moving, and he may have thought it was a stump. I was so surprised at it that I was not scared, and watched them as they went tearing over the prairie. There were four of them. I will never forget those bulging eyes I looked into as it went over me. My sister, Margaret, who was in the house with mother told me many years later that mother saw it just as the buffalo was upon me, screamed and fainted, falling to the floor. I suppose she thought it was the end of her child.

Father always, on returning home would drive the rig as close to the side of the building as he could, leaving the wagon there. He had his reasons for so doing and the horses taken to the log stable at the rear, a short distance from the house.

Mother stepped outside one evening, but soon returned, saying: "Pa, there is something out there in the wagon! I put my hand out and felt fu-r-r!" She was short of breath from fright Father laid his newspaper aside, got up and lit the candle in the lantern, and went out to investigate; he returned in a short time, and Mother, still shaking with fright, said, "Jacob, what was it!" And Father smilingly answered, "Nothing but a couple of bears, taking a snooze. They'll do no harm." And in the early morning they were gone. And that's that. "Believe it or not," it certainly did happen. And someday we'll tell you another story and it no "pipe-dream" either.

This is all true, though it may seem 'fishy' to some at the present time. But when you remember the country was still new at this time you will understand. Family after family came, and soon there was a great change. People seemed to pour in. Iowa is a beautiful state, no getting around it.

Love it all. Mother

NEWSPAPER ARTICLES
Written by Mary E. Leaman

*A*RTICLE PUBLISHED IN THE CHARLES *City Press newspaper on Thursday, Feb. 1ˢᵗ, 1940 written by Mary E. Leaman:*

Tells of Raid of Morgan in the Civil War

Mrs. Mary E. Leaman, of 1308 Clark Street, has written an interesting account of one of Morgan's raids in the north during the civil war it was told her by her mother. The account was recalled by her reading, "Gone with the Wind," a story of the civil war from a southern standpoint. Mrs. Leaman's article is as follows:

Reading Margaret Mitchell's interesting and popular book, "Gone with the Wind," it's plain to see her sympathies were with the south, no doubt, and mostly for good reason, as both the north and south had their grievances, suffering at the outlawry of both Morgan and Jennison with the men they had rallied to their aid in their vicious plundering and murder.

Morgan's Raid

We will begin with Morgan, whose raid in Salem, Indiana, we are more familiar with, as mother's uncle, Jonas Berkey, it seemed was the target of their onslaught. Jonas was a law-abiding citizen, kind-hearted and loved by his acquaintances. He was reputed to be very wealthy, in the multi-millionaire class, not so numerous in this country in its earlier days.

His wealth has been accumulated through his thrift and good business judgment. Instead of hoarding his money it was used to create business in his home town, building mills and factories, thus giving work to many of his townsmen enabling them to provide a living for their families, and he deservingly prospered. He also established a number of stores; namely dry goods, clothing, crockery, jewelry and grocery. These businesses called for clerks, accountants, bookkeepers, etc. and the town and its inhabitants, were prospering, and uncle was making money.

Hear of His Coming
Here is Aunt Evelyn's story of the raid, as told to mother, who visited there in the seventies, a few years after the war:

"Word came that Morgan and his men were on their way to Salem, your uncle and I thought it best to provide plenty of food, knowing they would most likely be a hungry army of men and treat them in a friendly manner. Everything necessary was provided, several women were hired, and with our own help of both men and women we prepared to serve the horde on their arrival. Your uncle thought to meet them himself in a friendly manner and compromise with them. I had my doubts as to the success of this plan and feared for his safety, and made my plans to protect him."

Town in an Uproar
"The day came when the marauding army arrived in Salem. The town was in an uproar. People were excited and frightened. I asked your uncle to go with me to the basement and get something I wanted from the wine cellar. Unsuspectingly he did so, and went inside. I quickly slammed the heavy door, shut and locked it, putting the key in my pocket. He called out to me, "Evelyn, open this door," but I was deaf to his call, and fled up the stairway to find the yard filled with the marauding army, calling out."

"We want Berkey." Of course, I did not know where he was, and he could not be heard outside of his prison."

Neighbor Shot Down

"I began with the helpers passing out food to the hungry mob, and while doing so, one of our neighbor men passing through the yard was shot down before my eyes, for no cause whatever. Just that morning he had been there talking with Jonas, and I thought the same thing would have happened to Jonas had I not locked him up.

They began their work of destruction and pillage, and I knew there should be some way provided to give Jonas a chance to compromise with them as soon as possible. I managed to get word to his lawyer that he was needed. He came immediately and was given the chance to confer with Jonas as to the best plan in meeting their demands. After talking the matter over Jonas decided to give the lawyer full charge, using his own judgment. They demanded the payment of $5,000 in cash from each factory, mill and store, to save the buildings from destruction by fire. This was after looting each place of all valuables and destroying what they did not carry off. Prior to this they had taken blankets and other articles from the woolen mill sufficient for the entire army."

Destroy Fine Goods

"They took from the dry goods store, bolts of the finest silks and velvets, carried them outside where their army on horseback was waiting, and threw them on the ground in front of the waiting horsemen. The leaders with one end of goods in their hands started their horses, and as the goods unwound they were trampled by the horses following.

After looting the jewelry store, carrying away with them all of the most valuable jewelry, they destroyed what they could not carry away. The last thing they helped themselves to was the family carriage, and a valuable span of horses a silver mounted harness and all that goes with a fine turnout. We hated most of all the loss of the horses as we were greatly attached to them. The last of the spoils enabled Morgan to leave town in a dignified manner, as became the leader of a notorious gang."

On returning from her visit, mother related to us the above account of all her aunt told her of their experiences during the Morgan raid, and we never forgot it.

It all came back to us when we read the book, "Gone with the Wind."

Article published in Charles City, Iowa newspaper in 1940, written by Mary E. Leaman:

Tells of The Raids of Jennison

Mrs. Mary Leaman, 1308 Clark Street, who recently, through the columns of the Press, told of Morgan and his outlaw band during the civil war, tells below of Colonel Jennison. These accounts were recalled by her after reading, "Gone with the Wind." The Jennison episode follows:

We record the doings of Jennison, called Colonel by his followers. He was a Federal, a Union man, but of the same stripe as the notorious Morgan. He was destroying property, robbing his hapless victims and murdering many. Like Morgan's men, they were a band of outlaws. Neither party had enlisted in their country's service, and of course there was no army discipline and this gave them a chance to gratify their brutal instincts.

A Wisconsin Man

Charlie Jennison was a Wisconsin man. In his boyhood, during his early years, he lived with his father on a small acreage. His mother was dead and he was his father's housekeeper. They kept a cow and a few chickens. His father left home each morning after breakfast, with his horse and buggy, not returning until evening. Charlie washed the dishes, made the bed, and tidied up the rooms, fed and watered the chickens, gathered the eggs, and then his duties were finished until time to prepare the evening meal. Too monotonous for an active boy, to spend the day by himself and he would mount the cow in lieu of a horse, and here he would come to our house running the poor cow, shouting and waving his cap.

Treated Kindly

Mother's heart went out to this motherless boy and she always treated him kindly. He remained at our house until time to start home and prepare their supper. Before he left, mother placed in his pockets whatever dainties she might have, cookies, doughnuts, etc. Bossy enjoyed these visits, feasting on the nice prairie grass, and having fresh water to drink, as well as an occasional treat of something extra.

Shocks Southerner

Years later, in 1904, we went to Indian Territory and our nearest neighbors were a southern family, very nice people they were. Each Sunday afternoon Mr. S. same to our house for a visit with my husband. On one of these visits something which had occurred during the civil war was spoken of and I became interested in their conversation, and thoughtlessly said something not so complimentary of the south. The memory of the experiences of mother's uncle's family during the Morgan raid in Salem, Indiana, was still in my memory, and for the moment I forgot that Mr. S. was a southerner. A sad, shocked look overspread his face for a moment, and he said, "Pardon me, Mrs.

Leaman, there are always two sides to be considered. As you must know, I am a southerner and if you care to hear an experience of mine during the civil war I will relate it."

Southerern Chivalry
Of course, I was ready to listen and apologized for what I had so thoughtlessly said. He said: "Let us forget it, there is no ill feeling whatever; I understand your feelings in this matter." Dismissing the subject with a smile and I felt for a moment like a whipped cur. The chivalry of a southern gentleman toward a woman far surpasses that of a northerner. His attitude is one of reverence and politeness. Mr. S.'s story follows:

Mr. S. Tells His Story
"Father owned a large plantation and had many slaves, fine buildings, and the finest of stocks. His horses were his special pride, fine animals, unsurpassed anywhere, and all else was in accordance.

After the Emancipation Proclamation father told his slaves they now were free to go anywhere they chose, that no longer could he hold them. But they were not ready to accept of their freedom, and preferred remaining in their cabins, which afforded them shelter, and continued their work as heretofore. They planted the usual crops, made gardens, cared for stock and poultry, setting the hens to raise more chickens and looked after the fruit trees, now loaded with an abundance of fruit. Everything on the plantation was very promising.

Jennison Suddenly Comes
In the midst of this placid and promising scene there came suddenly one day, Colonel Jennison and his band of outlaws. They began ordering mother and sister around in the most brutal manner, demanding food be cooked for this army of men, and it must be the best the place afforded. There was depletion of the poultry, besides butchering some of the finest of the cattle, and

ordering that the beef be cooked for them. The darkies* worked like beavers in answer to their demands. I was a boy of nine years of age at this time, and was so badly frightened at the appearance of this army of men I had hidden. Whether they might have harmed me had I been discovered I do not know, but the slaves were safe. They burned all the buildings except the house; they spared that perhaps because after brutally mistreating mother and sister, they left them lying helpless on the floor, bound hand and foot with the cords cutting into the flesh.

Hang His Father
They had taken father outside the house, and hung him to a limb of a tree in the yard. The horses with saddles, bridles, blankets, etc., were taken from the barn and it was then set on fire. They destroyed the crops, took all the fruit from the trees, placed it in sacks and carried it away with them. Everyone laid low until they were out of sight and then activities began. Mother had succeeded in freeing her hands from the cords, and released her feet; she was then able to release sister. Her next move was to go outside and learn what happened to father. She did not scream nor faint, there was no time for that, and mother was a brave woman. She must get him down from the tree with the help of the terrified darkies.* This was soon accomplished and laying him on the ground the rope was removed from his neck by mother who was on her knees by his side. She placed her hand on his side and found his heart was still faintly beating. She began rubbing him vigorously, and lifting his arms above, calling for water and towels, restoratives she kept in the house in case of emergency. She bathed him with warm water and I think alcohol, if I remember. He finally showed some signs of life and was carried into the house and placed on the bed, mother remaining constantly by his side.

Slowly Recovers
A physician was then called from town, and he slowly recovered, though was never very strong bodily afterward; the ordeal had been too much and he lived

but a few years, a quiet, peaceful life. The war was over, and the people of the war-torn south where the fighting had been had plenty to do to rebuild their burned homes and reclaim their land from the effects of its baptism of shot and shell, for more than four years."

*In the 1940's this terminology seemed to be acceptable in the newspaper.

NEWSPAPER EXCERPTS FROM CHARLES CITY PRESS
Regarding Mary E. Leaman

"EIGHTY-EIGHT YEARS OLD – Mrs. Mary Leaman, who has written many articles about Charles City in the early days, was 88 years of age Friday. To mark the occasion, many callers extended their felicitations to her at the home of Mr. and Mrs. C.A. Danforth, 1308 Clark Street, her son-in-law and daughter, with whom she resides.

Local members of the family spent some of the time with her, and Mrs. Leaman's daughter and granddaughter, Mrs. Fay Stoeber and Mrs. Helen Behm of Mason City, were present for the birthday dinner. She received nice remembrances.

A longtime resident of this community, she still enjoys excellent health. She does not spend much time writing as she once did, but reads a great deal. Mrs. Leaman came here in a covered wagon as a child with her parents, when this side was the village of Freeman.

She is a cousin of the late Lillian Russell, famous stage beauty."

(Excerpt from Newspaper: Sept. 30, 1927)

"MRS. LEAMAN REWRITES SONG FROM MEMORY – Mrs. Mary E. Leaman of this city has contributed a permanent record of an early Iowa song at the request of her brother-in-law, Edward E. Smith of Minneapolis who was asked by Mark Sullivan, nationally known writer for the song, 'Iowa Counties.'

About the year 1861, Mrs. Leaman attended school on the west side of the river when her teacher, J. Chester Whitney, composed and set to music verses reciting the name of all of the counties in Iowa. It was sung each morning during the opening exercises and few of the pupils attending that school are living today.

Mrs. Leaman has re-written the song from memory and it has been forwarded by Mr. Smith to Mr. Sullivan who will use it in his second volume of 'Our Times. The following is a copy of that song:

Iowa Counties

THE COUNTIES OF IOWA

By: J. Cheston Whitney

Our home is in Iowa,
Westward toward the setting sun,
Just between two mighty rivers,
Where the flowing waters run;
It has towns and it has cities,
It has many noble streams,
It has ninety-nine counties,
And we'll join to sing their names.

Lyon, Osceola, Dickinson,
Where the Spirit Lake we see;
Emmet, Kossuth, Winnebago,
Worth, with its Lake Albert Lea;
Mitchell, Howard, Winneshiek,
And Allamakee so fine,
Make eleven northern counties
On the Minnesota line.

Clayton, Dubuque, Jackson, Clinton,
Together with Scott and Muscatine,
Lee, Louisa and Des Moines,
On the eastern line is seen;
Van Buren, Davis, Appanoose,
Decatur, Ringgold, Wayne, we spy;
Taylor, Page and Fremont, that

On Missouri's border lie.

Pottawattamie, Harrison, Mills,
Monona, Woodbury, Plymouth, Sioux,
Are all the counties that around
The border of our State we view.
Next we point you to O'Brien,
Palo Alto too, and Clay,
Hancock, Cerro Gordo, Floyd,
Now see Chickasaw, I pray.

Fayette, Bremer, Butler, Franklin,
Next upon the map we see;
Wright and Humboldt, Pocahontas,
Buena Vista, Cherokee,
Ida, Sac, Calhoun and Webster,
Hamilton, with names so rare;
Next is Hardin, Grundy, Black Hawk,
And Buchanan, Delaware.

Jones, Linn, Benton, Tama, Marshall,
Story, Crawford, Carroll, Boone,
(Let us not your patience weary,
We shall have them all told soon,)
Cedar, Greene, Johnson, Iowa,
With Powesheik by the same;
Here is Jasper, Polk and Dallas,
Names of Presidential fame.

Guthrie, Audubon and Shelby,
Cass and Madison, Adair,
Warren, Marion and Mahaska,
And Keokuk, too, is there:
Henry, Jefferson and Wapello,
Monroe, Washington we missed;
Lucas, Clarke, Union, Adams.
And Montgomery fills the list.

(Source: History of Floyd County, Iowa, 1882)

FAMILY PHOTOGRAPHS

One of the Leaman homes in Charles City, Iowa.

The Leonard Hotel in Charles City, Iowa.

Catherine Leonard, mother of Mary Eliza Leaman.

Mary E. Leaman with a canine friend in the 1930's.

Mary's Story

**Grandma Mary with her granddaughters,
Mary Jane and Betty June.**

Charles D. Leaman with grandson, Charles E. Gilligan fishing on the Oregon coast.

Mary's Story

Mary and her daughter, Madge Danforth.

**Mary with her son,
Charles D. Leaman, and his wife Lucile**

The Leamans, plus one dog, are looking forward to getting to Washington State!

The Leaman's Airedale dog, Jiggs rode shotgun on the running board of the car as they drove to Longview from Iowa. Charles put an extra board on the outside of the car for Jiggs to ride on. After purchasing gasoline one day, 30 miles down the road one of the girls said, "Where's Jiggs?" as he was not on the running board. Charles returned to the service station and found their beloved dog waiting patiently

The Leaman Café Lunch Cart at the Paul Bunyan Days in Longview, Washington

```
SUNDAY                    DECEMBER 6Ø, 1942


                    DINNERS

CREAM OF TOMATO SOUP   OR GRAPEFRUIT OR
                            TOMATO JUICE

ROAST YOUNG TOM TURKEY WITH
        STUFFING AND CRANBERRY SAUCE.. 75
ROAST SIRLOIN OF BEEF-BROWN GRAVY... 60
BREADED VEAL CUTLETS-CREAM GRAVY.... 60
ROAST LEG OF PORK-APPLE SAUCE....... 60
FRIED FRESH SIDE PORK WITH
                    APPLE RINGS.... 60

              * * * *
```

Menu from Leaman's Lunch in Longview, WA

The Leaman girls in their early teens.

The Leaman Girls a few years later!

Lucile and Charles D. Leaman (son of Mary E. Leaman) in Longview, WA

Excerpts from Article in the Longview Daily News Business Section:

Back in 1926 the Leaman family, consisting of Mr. and Mrs. Charles D. Leaman and their 2 daughters, Betty June and Mary Jane, packed their things into the family automobile (Desoto) and set out for the Pacific coast on a pleasure trip. It was just supposed to be a trip for a few months, but they've never moved back, and they would not, if Mr. Leaman has anything to say about it.

They arrived in Tacoma and visited his brother, Roy and wife, who were living there. After seeing advertisements for Longview in several states along the way and seeing it advertised again while in Tacoma as this beautiful "planned city" they decided to move on to Longview and live. They bought a small lunch counter establishment and opened for business. It flourished and soon they decided to move down the street to a larger food restaurant at 1113

Commerce and called it Leaman's Lunch. In the front window Charlie placed plants, with live frogs hopping around!

Charlie D. Leaman was the cook; Lucile and eventually Jane and Betty were the waitresses. The food was good and Charlie was known as "Chili Charlie" and kept the secret recipe in his wallet. The girls went to Kessler School. The Leaman's lived in several houses and eventually in the Tibbet's Apartments close to their restaurant. Jane and Betty Leaman graduated from R.A. Long High School in Longview. Jane remained in Longview, married and started a family and Betty returned to Tacoma to marry and start her family.

Charlie and Lucile sold the restaurant and moved to Seal Rock, Oregon in 1945. Purchasing seven acres on the beach with a trailer park attached, which kept them busy throughout retirement. The Leaman clan—children, grandchildren and extended family spent many happy days on the beach; and to this day there are still Leaman's descending the cliffs and enjoying the beach.

Sample of Mary's Handwriting

Charles City, Iowa
March 1st, 1929.

Dear Charlie & Family:—

Forty-one years ago today another boy was added to the Leaman flock. And didn't he make the "welkin ring" with his cries! Grandma Allen said: "I have taken care of 150 babies and this is the worst one of all. You will just have to get another nurse; one can not do it all, night and day." The echo of those cries did not entirely cease for three months, and after that I had the best baby ever. And I still wonder what could have ailed him. But you have been lots of comfort to mother, and we don't regret the extra work and worry you made them. May you live to a good old age and a comfort to Lucile & the girls. God bless my boy. Lovingly, Mother

FAMILY OBITUARIES

Obituary for Mary's Father, Jacob Leonard:

JACOB LEONARD

Jacob Leonard, known to everybody in this city by the familiar name of "Uncle Jake," died of heart disease, steps from his home. J. H. Owens and S. B. Ball were nearby when he fell, but he was dead when they reached him. The points of the following biography are gleaned from the Floyd County Histories.

Jacob Leonard was born near Bedford, Lawrence County, Indiana, on December 12, 1819. When he was about two years old, his parents moved to Monroe County and settled on a farm. He was reared and educated at that place, and was married there on December 20, 1842, to Miss Catherine Berkey, who survives him. Of the nine children born of this union, seven are living: William H. of Chicago; Margaret A. wife of William Gange of this place; Mary E., wife of Charles W. Leaman of this place; Kate, wife of Joseph Flannigan; Agnes, wife of Frank Gilbert of Chicago; Esther, wife of E. E. Smith of Baltimore and Clara A., wife of Frank Gleason of Grinnell. After his marriage, Mr. Leonard farmed in Monroe County, Indiana until 1843, and then taught until 1847, when he went to Green County, Wisconsin, continuing in the same occupation there. In the spring of 1856 he came to Charles City moving his family here the following year. He farmed, teamed and engaged in draying until 1875, he opened a grocery store, which he sold a short time afterward, and brought the Cleveland House. In October, 1879, he built the Leonard House near the C. M. and St. Paul Railroad Depot and for about five years he was its genial host and a popular landlord. It was a two-story building, containing fifteen sleeping rooms, parlors, dining room, office and kitchen—all fitted-up in good style. Mr. Leonard showed his guests every attention. He was elected justice of the peace for two-years, but resigned the office before the expiration of his term. Politically he is a strong supporter of the Republican Party.

For a number of years he has been in poor health, but the end was none the less unexpected. Mr. Leonard was one of the kindest hearted of men, and every man, woman and child in the city was his friend and will mourn his death. The funeral took place Friday morning, the services being conducted by Rev. C. S. Dean. His son, William H., was present from Chicago, and his son-in-law, Archie Reed from Janesville, Wisconsin. The attendance was very large, especially of the older people who have been for years his intimates.

Newspaper article regarding 100th birthday of Mary Eliza's mother:

MRS. LEONARD HAS REACHED CENTURY MARK

Mrs. Catherine Leonard is one hundred years old today. Mrs. Leonard is the mother of Mrs. William Gange and Mrs. Charles Leaman of this city, and grandmother of Mrs. W. B. Johnson.

She left this city about four years ago to make her home with her daughter, Mrs. E. M. Smith in Minneapolis.

Mrs. Leonard is one of the pioneer residents of this city and county, and five generations of her descendants are living.

Mrs. Leonard is reported to be in very poor health.

The following is a short sketch of the life of Mrs. Leaman and birthday greetings from her children.

Mrs. Catherine Leonard was one of the early pioneers who with her late husband, Jacob Leonard and their three eldest children, arrived in the village of St. Charles, (now Charles City) June 16, 1857.

"She bravely met all inconveniences of early pioneer life of such as the present generation cannot conceive. She did her bit in those early days to make the most of what she had and together with her late husband and other pioneer women and men built a home in this community, then a wilderness, remaining here until too feeble to keep up a home. She went to Minneapolis about six years ago, and she has since made her home with youngest of her remaining daughters, Mrs. E. E. Smith."

"Five of her nine children remain, who rejoice in the possessions of God's choicest blessings, 'A Good Mother.' With her are five generations—namely twenty-seven grandchildren, fifteen great-grandchildren and five great-great-grandchildren."

Birthday Greetings

Birthday greetings to our mother, who passes the one hundredth milestone today, August 23, 1926. Your children and grandchildren would pay you homage, Mother Dear, for many years of faithful service and devotion to each one who has loved you more with the passing years, and may we, when the shade of life's evening gathers round us, be found waiting with a faith and hope like yours and having lived so good a life. Lovingly your children: Mrs. Margaret Gange, Mrs. Mary Leaman, Mrs. Catherine Hamilton, Mrs. Agnes Gilbert and Mrs. Esther Smith.

Obituary for Mary's mother, Catherine Leonard:

CATHERINE LEONARD DIES TWO DAYS AFTER HER 100TH BIRTHDAY
N. W. Pioneer's Life Ebbs After Reaching Century Mark, Her Goal for Years
CONDITION CALLED GOOD AFTER PARTY MONDAY
Received 40 Callers on Birthday at Home of Daughter, Despite Slight Illness

Just two days after celebrating her 100th birthday, Mrs. Catherine Berkey Leonard, a northwest pioneer, died today at the home of her daughter, Mrs. E. E. Smith, 2109 Blaisdell Avenue.

Monday, Mrs. Leonard lay at her daughter's home while a steady stream of callers payed their respects. Last night Mrs. Leonard murmured *"I am so tired."* Then early today, she died, the goal on which her heart had been set for years achieved.

When Mrs. Leonard first came to Charles City, Iowa, in a covered wagon, their log cabin was the only house for several miles around. She often told how at night they had to board up the windows to keep out the wild animals.

When Mrs. Leonard was a young woman there were no stores at which to buy the things a housewife needs. She told of making her own cornstarch, baking powder and soap. When she got her first candle molds she thought she was the richest woman in the community. Often buying was a case of barter and she related how once she traded some geese for sheep. Then she sheered the sheep, spun the yarn herself and after a neighbor had woven the cloth; Mrs. Leonard made it into clothing by hand.

Despite an illness which sent her to bed six weeks ago; the woman who believed that *"More people die by rusting out than by working,"* had clung tenaciously to life. She wanted to live to be 100 years old—and when her birthday passed she seems to crumble-up completely, relatives said today.

Buried in Iowa Friday

Friday at Charles City, Iowa, where she lived in a tiny log cabin years ago when the northwest was a wilderness spotted with a few pioneer settlements, Mrs. Leonard will be buried.

Born in Jackson County, Indiana, Mrs. Leonard pioneered in three states—northern Indiana, southern Wisconsin and Iowa. Six years ago she came to Minneapolis to live with her daughter, Mrs. Smith. In the 100 years of her life, Mrs. Leonard saw many great men come and go, saw the United States fight and win three wars, saw the wilderness in the northwest vanish, and the telephone, the electric light, the automobile and the airplane come.

Mary Eliza Leaman's newspaper obituary:

DEATH TAKES PIONEER OF CITY

Mrs. Mary E. Leaman, age 90 years and seven months, passed away Sunday morning at the home of her daughter, Mrs. C. A. Danforth 1308 E. Clark Street. Mrs. Leaman had made her home with her daughter for the past twenty five-years. She was one of the early settlers of Charles City coming with her parents to this city in a covered wagon at the age of three years. She was a member of the First Christian Church.

Mary Eliza Leonard was born to Jacob and Catherine Leonard April 17th, 1854 at Albany, Wisconsin. She came with her parents to Charles City as a small child and on April 15, 1871 she united to C. W. Leaman at Waverly, Iowa. To this union were born seven children, three of whom survive. They are Charles Leaman of Longview, Washington; Mrs. Fay Stoeber of Oakland, California; and Mrs. C. A. Danforth of Charles City. Children preceding their mother in death were Mrs. Vera Carbiener; Roy Leaman; Mrs. Doris Malone and Miss Myrtle Leaman. Mr. Leaman preceded his wife in death on February 13, 1912. There are eleven grandchildren, twelve great-grandchildren and one great-great-grandchild surviving, also one sister, Mrs. E. E. Smith of West Hartford, Conn.

Mary E. Leaman passed away on December 22, 1944 and funeral services will be held Wednesday afternoon at 2:00 o'clock at the Hauser Funeral Home. The Rev. A. A. Burr, pastor of the first Christian Church will officiate. Interment will be made in Riverside Cemetery.

GENEALOGY

Jacob Leonard
B: Dec. 12, 1819 in Bedford, Indiana
D: Oct. 11, 1888 in Charles City, Iowa
Father of Mary Eliza

Catherine Berkey Leonard
B: August 23, 1826 in North Carolina
D: August 25, 1926 in Charles City, Iowa
Mother of Mary Eliza

Mary Eliza Leonard Leaman
B: April 17, 1854 in Albany, Wisconsin
D: December 22, 1944 in Charles City, Iowa

Charles W. Leaman
B: December 1846 in Rockford, Illinois
(Married **Mary Eliza** on April 15, 1871 in Waverly, Iowa)
D: February 13, 1912 in Tulsa, Oklahoma
Husband of Mary Eliza

Charles D. Leaman
B: March 1, 1888 in Charles City, Iowa
D: August 5, 1965 in Seal Rock, Oregon
Son of Mary Eliza

Lucile Hollis Leaman
B: December 23, 1891 in Clay Center, Kansas
D: April 18, 1965 Longview, Washington
Daughter-in-law of Mary Eliza, wife of Charles D.

Mary Jane Leaman
B: January 12, 1915 in Charles City, Iowa
D: November 20, 1976 in Tacoma, Washington
Granddaughter of Mary Eliza, daughter of Charles and Lucile

Edward Joseph Gilligan
B: August 16, 1910 in Estelline, South Dakota
D: January 19, 1969 in Longview, Washington
Grandson-in-law of Mary Eliza, husband of Mary Jane

Eileen Susan Gilligan McKeag Carlyle
B: December 5, 1942 in Longview, Washington
Great-Granddaughter of Mary Eliza
Compiler of *"MARY'S STORY"*

NOTE: *Genealogy contains information for this branch of the family ONLY to show direct connection from Mary Eliza Leaman to her descendant, Eileen Carlyle. Eileen compiled this book from gathered information saved from Mary Eliza's hand-written memoirs, personal correspondence, and newspaper articles.*

EILEEN GILLIGAN MCKEAG CARLYLE IS the great-granddaughter of Mary Eliza Leaman. It had been Mary's wish to have all of her writings compiled into a book. Due to life circumstances and lack of a typewriter, she never brought her dream to completion. Eileen's own mother and grandmother carried the makings of this memoir in dusty boxes, files and drawers throughout the years. Eileen finally decided that she had to complete this task for her great-grandmother. At the age of 75, Eileen is at last publishing **"MARY'S STORY."**

Eileen spent many summer's visiting her grandparents, Charles D. and Lucile Leaman, at the beach in Seal Rock, Oregon. As a child and young adult she would often ride the Greyhound Bus from Longview, Washington; she would then be met by her grandparents at the mailbox on Hwy 101 at the Seal Rock Trailer Park.

Eileen was born in Longview, Washington and has lived her adult life in Puyallup, Washington where she raised her own family. Eileen enjoys traveling, photography, card games, time with family & writing.

Made in the USA
Columbia, SC
20 December 2017